Frederick James Johnson

The beloved disciple

a sermon preached in Wesley-Chapel

Frederick James Johnson

The beloved disciple
a sermon preached in Wesley-Chapel

ISBN/EAN: 9783744744805

Printed in Europe, USA, Canada, Australia, Japan

Cover: Foto ©Lupo / pixelio.de

More available books at **www.hansebooks.com**

The Beloved Disciple.

A SERMON

PREACHED IN WESLEY-CHAPEL, LINCOLN, JANUARY 26TH, 1868,

ON THE DEATH OF THE

REV. JOHN HANNAH, D.D.

WITH A

BIOGRAPHICAL SKETCH

OF THE DECEASED.

BY

FREDERICK J. JOBSON, D.D.

LONDON:
66, PATERNOSTER-ROW.
MDCCCLXVIII.

TO THE

𝔚𝔢𝔰𝔩𝔢𝔶𝔞𝔫 𝔐𝔢𝔱𝔥𝔬𝔡𝔦𝔰𝔱𝔰 𝔬𝔣 𝔱𝔥𝔢 ℭ𝔦𝔱𝔶 𝔬𝔣 𝔏𝔦𝔫𝔠𝔬𝔩𝔫

THE FOLLOWING DISCOURSE,

DELIVERED ON

THE DEATH OF A CHRISTIAN MINISTER

WHOM THEY

LOVED, HONOURED, AND REVERED,

IS RESPECTFULLY AND FRATERNALLY INSCRIBED

BY THEIR FELLOW-CITIZEN.

PREFACE.

Friendship has its obligations as well as its privileges. Hence, when my Methodist fellow-citizens requested me to improve for them the death of my beloved friend, Dr. Hannah, in his native city, I felt, at once, that it was my duty to comply. The same sense of obligation impels me to respond to their further request, and to publish this Sermon and Memoir.

Ordinarily, no apology for an unfinished literary production ought to avail with readers, who have a full claim upon an author for his best performances. But, in addition to the very brief time necessarily intervening between death and a funeral-sermon, it must in this case be named, that severe personal and family affliction, as well as pressing daily duties, left but few hours for preparing the following Discourse and its accompanying Biographical Sketch.

If, to general readers, the contents of these pages should seem too free and local in some of their references, let it be remembered that the Discourse was delivered in Dr. Hannah's native city, to an audience comprising those who had known him from his youth up, and who had grateful recollections of his early and devout association with themselves in the services of Methodism.

In conclusion, the author would add, that he will be thankful to find that this fragmentary and familiar Sketch of one so worthy of the most honourable memorial is made available in supplying any facts and incidents for a more full and finished Biography by an abler hand.

F. J. J.

21, Highbury-Place, London, N.,
January, 1868.

SERMON.

JOHN XXI. 20.

"THE DISCIPLE WHOM JESUS LOVED."

How superior, in force and beauty of significance, are the titles and distinctions given by the Divine Being in the Scriptures to His servants, compared with the appendages affixed by the world and the Church to the names of those whom they delight to honour! Men strain their ingenuity for high-sounding terms with which to immortalize their favourites; and style them, "the sublime," "the magnificent," "the great," "the heroic," "the golden-mouthed," "the venerable," "the judicious." But how vastly inferior are all such boasted titles to the simple and dignified descriptions which the Almighty has given in His word of those in whom He had special delight! How little and mean are such human epithets, for instance, to the inspired declarations concerning Enoch and Noah, that they "walked with God;"—of Abraham, that he was "called the Friend of God;"—of Moses, "whom the Lord knew face to face;"—of David, that he was "the man after His own heart;"—of Daniel, that he was "greatly beloved;"—and of Nathanael, that he was "an Israelite indeed, in whom is no guile." These, and others that might be named, are each and all higher titles than any to be found in mere human history. But the title which is three times claimed by St. John in his own Gospel is more beautiful and more honourable than any of them,—"the disciple whom Jesus loved." To be loved by the Saviour, by God incarnate, by the holiest, the gentlest, and the most lovable of all beings,—there can be no title or distinction so precious and desirable as this.

I do not fear the charge of presumption in selecting this text of honourable appellation for the apostle St. John as the basis of observation upon the character of our deceased father and friend. Mingling, as I have been privileged to do, with Christian people and Christian ministers of almost every clime and every name, I have never been personally associated with any man who seemed to me so fully to represent, anew, "the disciple whom Jesus loved," as DOCTOR HANNAH. His character seemed, most remarkably, to be cast in the same mould and type as that of St. John. Seventeen hundred years have passed since the beloved disciple fell asleep in Christ at Ephesus; and our venerated friend and fellow-citizen passed to his eternal rest only a few days ago. The times, also, in which the apostle lived differed, in many respects, from the times in which our departed fellow-townsman wrought out his pilgrimage from earth to heaven. But, notwithstanding these differences of age and circumstances, the resemblance, in the main features of their spiritual characters, is so strong and marked, as to render the service I have to perform easy, and, I trust, profitable. I shall not, however, attempt any set and formal parallel, as if I aimed to become a Christian Plutarch. Nor shall I forget the distinctive difference of one "called to be an apostle" and a minister "separated unto the Gospel of God" in the nineteenth century of our Lord. I shall simply endeavour to direct your attention to some of the more evident points of resemblance to the beloved disciple in the religious character of him who has so recently passed from the church militant on earth to the church triumphant in heaven. And I humbly hope and earnestly pray that the fact thus set before us—of one of our own generation, one familiarly known by us, having largely possessed the excellence of the very holiest apostle—may stimulate us both in our aspirations and endeavours for personal holiness.

1. Observe, then, that "the disciple whom Jesus loved" gave DEVOUT AND REVERENT ATTENTION TO HIS MASTER'S TEACHING. The

very term "disciple," which means literally *scholar*, signifies this. And how reverently attentive St. John was to the teaching of Christ may be seen in his affectionate remembrance of what the Saviour was, and in his full and minute record of what the Saviour said. No one of the Twelve has left us such a reverent and full portraiture of Christ as that which we owe to the loving limner, St. John. The mind of the apostle seems to have been open, with the most unreserved confidence and trust, to receive his Lord's teaching. From the time when the Baptist pointed Jesus out, at Bethabara, as God's chosen and appointed Sin-offering for mankind, John had no doubt or misgiving of the Divine mission of Christ as the Messiah. At once he would seem to have relied upon the Lamb of God for the taking away of his sins, and to have given himself up, heart and mind, for learning the great truths which Jesus came to make known. Ever after that memorable day by the Jordan, when, from being the disciple of the Baptist, he became the disciple of Jesus, and abode with Him by express invitation, John attended, with open and ready soul, to receive without cavil and without reserve whatever the Divine Master vouchsafed to communicate. Whatever doubts or misgivings other disciples might have concerning the Saviour, the "loving disciple" had none. John had not to ask, "Who art Thou?" or, "If Thou *art* the Christ, tell us plainly." He believed with the fullest confidence of a devout soul that Jesus was the Son of God and the true Messiah; and he opened freely his mind to receive the great Master's teaching.

And what a lovable mind was that of St. John! How artless and child-like in its simplicity, and yet how wondrously capable of the loftiest thoughts! How calmly and surely it soared up to the Father in heaven; and back to the past solitude of the eternal abyss before anything was made! The eagle, selected by old painters, is, indeed, the true emblem of John the Divine, in the height and sweep of his Gospel. The "Omnific Word"

—the *Logos* which confused the thoughts of Plato—the Evangelist John traced, not in relation to human genealogies, as do Matthew and Luke, but in His Divine and eternal Sonship, to the very bosom of the Father. John asserts most positively his Master's Divinity; declaring that He was in the beginning, before creation of any kind, that He was the Creator of all things, and that He is the light and life of men. John proclaims his Lord's incarnation; and affirms that "the Word was made flesh, and dwelt among us, (and we beheld His glory, the glory as of the only begotten of the Father,) full of grace and truth." And then, as if radiant with the heavenly light shed upon him by the Divine Teacher, and thoroughly convinced that Jesus had come from God, and was God incarnate, the "loving disciple" set himself to record the very words of the Saviour, as they fell from His lips; and to record the most touching incidents in His life, death, and resurrection.

I repeat it, and repeat it gratefully,—No

one of the Twelve has given us so full and reverent a portraiture of Christ as St. John. Without his Gospel, we should miss much of the minute details of our Lord's character and life. Think of John's picture of the marriage in Cana of Galilee, where Jesus was present to sanction and to sanctify the wedded union of man and woman, and to enrich the marriage-feast by His words and works. Think of John's most valuable record of Christ's discourse by night with Nicodemus; and of the precious communications made therein on inward renewal of man's nature by the Spirit, on God's inexpressible love for a perishing world, and on the eternal life to be obtained by man through faith in a lifted-up Saviour. Think of John's beautiful pictures of the Saviour by the Well of Samaria, and at the Pool of Bethesda. Think of the marvellous words of Christ which John records relative to the resurrection unto life which they shall experience that have done good; and of the resurrection unto damnation which they shall experience that have done evil. Think of John's wondrous picture of verisimilitude — the healing of the blind man; and of that sweetest masterpiece of all family-pictures—John's description of the household at Bethany, and of the love of Jesus for Martha, Mary, and Lazarus. Think of the parable of the "Good Shepherd," and its lessons, recorded solely by the fourth Evangelist. Think of those tenderest, and most precious to the believer, of all the pages of the New Testament—John's relation of the Passover-Feast, and his rehearsal of that sublime and heart-touching Farewell Address to the disciples: that superhuman discourse of love and consolation which John himself is recorded to have often repeated from memory in his extreme old age. Think of John's relation of the agony in the garden, the crucifixion, the resurrection, the appearances to the early visitors of the sepulchre, the appeal to Thomas, the showing of Jesus to His disciples by the lake of Galilee, the restoration of Peter to his place in the apostleship, and the final call of that apostle to follow Christ;

and then say if John had not been reverently attentive to his Master's teaching, and if he has not given the fullest and most highly-wrought portraiture of the Saviour. The last Evangelist—the "loving disciple"—has filled up the Gospel outline, put into it the most tender and compassionate features, and made it stand forth in its own simple majesty and Divine impressiveness.

Jesus deeply loved this simple, open, receptive mind of St. John, and rewarded it by fulness of communication. Who has pleasure in being misunderstood, or in being unappreciated? The Saviour felt the pain of being in a questionable position; and said, "Have I been so long with you, and yet hast thou not known Me, Philip?" But He had not to utter such words of tender and gentle reprehension to John. That disciple was a reverent, attentive scholar, who sat at the feet of Jesus, and heard His word; and therefore was "the disciple whom Jesus loved."

This *simple, open, receptive,* and *reverent*

nature was a prominent characteristic of our deceased father and friend. From the time when he first knew the truth as it is in Jesus, and received the call to follow Christ, he was devoutly and earnestly attentive to his Master's teachings. Having been blessed with Divine illumination, and having seen the glory of God in the face of Jesus Christ; having been born again, and having experienced, like John, that the blood of Jesus Christ cleanseth from all sin, so that he could confidently exclaim, "Beloved, now *are we* the sons of God;" he had no misgivings on essential, saving truth; and he had no reserve in proclaiming it. His theology was not based upon the speculations of men, which may shift, as loose uncertain sands with wind and tide. It rested on the Divine word, and was corroborated by his own experience. With what bright illumination, and with what glowing delight, did Dr. Hannah expatiate upon the Divinity of the Son of God, upon His incarnation in human flesh, and upon His teaching and work as a Saviour! All who remember his ministry will bear witness to this; and all the Students favoured with his Theological Lectures will give like testimony concerning this excellence in the character of his teaching as a Christian Professor. While simple and unconstrained in his style and forms of expression, yet what Divine illumination appeared in his teaching! How certain the knowledge we took of him that he had been with Jesus! How fully assured we were that he had taken truth from Christ's own words, and not from the subtleties of human reasoning!

He was a student who pursued large doctrinal inquiries, and was not unacquainted with the scholastic theology of the Middle Ages. But the Divine word was the Fountain of Truth to which he continually went; and it was for him the infallible standard of judgment for all he read and heard besides. His pure love for revealed truth was beautiful. The jargon of polemics neither moved nor attracted him. While able to discriminate the different shades of thought by controversialists, and to weigh their arguments, yet he could not bear the distraction occasioned by them. His copy of the New Testament, in its original language, or in Bengel's rendering, was his daily companion. He took it with him wherever he went, devoutly read it, and reverently received its revelations into a mind open, receptive, and tenacious, like the apostle John's. In this respect he, too, was "the disciple whom Jesus loved."

2. Further, "the disciple whom Jesus loved" evinced ARDENT AND AFFECTIONATE INTEREST IN HIS MASTER'S PERSON AND SERVICE. This was a strong and prominent feature in the apostle St. John. He clung to Jesus with more than a brother's affection. He was more than womanly in the tenderness and devotedness of his love. He was with Christ in the most private scenes, and on the most solemn and sacred occasions. He was with Him in the house of Jairus the ruler, where the dead was raised to life, and where

only two other favoured disciples were admitted. He was with Him on the Mount of Transfiguration, where the bright cloud overshadowed the enraptured witnesses, and where Jesus and His heavenly visitants spake of His decease to be accomplished at Jerusalem. He beheld the sorrowful scene of Bethany; and, with a heart full of emotion, compressed his description of the grief for His human friend, experienced by the perfect human nature of the Saviour, within two short words,—"Jesus wept." Indeed, he is the historian of the Saviour's tears. He drooped his pensive head on his Lord's bosom, as he heard of coming separation; and leaned upon that breast which, while heaving with surging sorrow for a sinful world, throbbed with sympathy for him and his fellow-apostles, about to be left, as they timidly thought, "comfortless." He was in the Garden of Gethsemane, where Jesus prayed in agony that bathed him in a sweat of blood. He saw his Master betrayed, bound, led away to judgment. He stood near the cross with the weeping women, when others had forsaken the Saviour and fled. He adhered to Him when even. Peter denied Him. He received, from the crucified and expiring Redeemer, Christ's own mother, as the most precious legacy, and as a dying token of the most confident love that could possibly be bequeathed to him. "And from that hour that disciple took her unto his own home," where, in the place of Jesus, he daily ministered to her with filial affection.

On learning that Jesus was risen from the dead, in his quick and ardent love, he outran Peter, and came first to the sepulchre, where, stooping down, he looked in. He was with the disciples who saw Jesus in the upper room. He saw Him again when Thomas was present; and has recorded how He who was alive from the dead was willing to have His wounds of crucifixion and of the soldier's spear re-opened, to dispel the doubts of the unbelieving disciple. He was on the Sea of Galilee when Jesus stood on the shore, and gave counsel to the hungry and weary disciples that filled their boat and nets with living loads; and, with the sharp-sighted intuition of love, beheld who the unknown stranger was, and said to Peter, "It is the Lord." He stood and heard the charge to Peter; and went forth to follow Christ at His command, patiently waiting for His coming again. When a lonely witness for the faith in the Isle of Patmos, he saw Jesus, the Alpha and the Omega, the first and the last; and exultantly heard Him proclaim, "I am He that liveth, and was dead; and, behold, I am alive for evermore."

He taught and governed the Church at Ephesus in love; and wrote Epistles overflowing with the tenderest affection,—Epistles which, in their simple and unconnected parts, are as the very spillings of his heart. He was so engrossed with the theme of love to Christ for what He had done, and for what He would do for those that believe in Him, that he refers to Him without so much as mentioning His name; knowing that Jesus would be apprehended by all who could exclaim, "We shall be like *Him*, for we shall see *Him* as *He* is." He pondered on the moral character of God until he compressed the whole Gospel into three short words, and gave expression, in a single sentence, to a truth that eternity will not exhaust or fully make known,—"God is love." In extreme old age, as an early historian relates, he used to repeat to the assembled church at Ephesus, day by day, fragments of the last discourses of the Saviour. And when he became so much enfeebled by years that he could no longer walk to the church, and teach connectedly, they who loved him carried him in a chair, and set him down in the midst of the congregation, where, in fatherly simplicity and affection,—being then one hundred years old,—he would stretch out his trembling hands, and say, "Little children, love one another." Undoubtedly John was, in spirit and disposition, tenderly affectionate. His Gospel, his Epistles, his conduct and words, all show this unmistakeably. And with the full ardour of his loving, sanctified nature he was attached to Christ's person and service. On this account, also, he was "the disciple whom Jesus loved."

It was so with our deceased fellow-citizen. *Affectionateness of disposition* was in him a strong characteristic. And with the full ardour of his loving nature he devoted himself to the person and service of Christ. Jesus was "all, and in all" to him. Jesus was "the Angel standing in the sun"—the very centre and source of light and life. His delight was to think of Christ, speak of Christ, and preach Him in all His offices and work. Who ever heard Dr. Hannah preach a Christless sermon? Who ever heard him preach generalities in philosophy, or mere morality, leaving Christ out of his sermon, or in a secondary place or position? Who ever knew him mock sinful, perishing men with eloquent harangues on what would be called, by some, "original and interesting subjects," but which left his hearers misinformed on the way of life and salvation? O no! they who heard DR. HANNAH preach must hear of Christ; hear of Christ, as the only way of salvation; hear of Christ, as in Peter's sermon on the day of Pentecost—at the beginning, the middle, and at the end of the sermon. If you heard him, you must hear of Christ crucified, Christ risen from the dead, Christ exalted, Christ enthroned. He loved Christ; and therefore must preach Him; and preach Him as made unto His people "wisdom, righteousness, sanctification, and redemption." He must preach Christ as the source and subject of exultant hope to all His followers. And with this strong and affectionate attachment to Christ, he loved Christ's cause, and sought by all possible means to extend Christ's name and glory upon the earth. In this respect, also, our departed friend was "the disciple whom Jesus loved."

3. Again, "the disciple whom Jesus loved" sought FULL AND COMPLETE CONFORMITY

TO HIS MASTER'S EXAMPLE. Who of the disciples is so like Christ as John? Tradition reports that there was close resemblance between the form and figure of St. John and Jesus; and when we picture for ourselves the face of John, we imagine in the countenance the same calm and pensive repose, the same thoughtful, unruffled brow, and the same sweet smile as on the face of Jesus. But tradition and imagination are uncertain grounds on which to rest. The moral and spiritual qualities of Jesus, however, John had in fullest and fairest attainment. His tender, plastic, receptive soul took the deepest and clearest impress of his Master's character. His pure heart enabled him to see God in Christ most clearly; and his calm, unruffled depth of love reflected the traits and features of the Saviour's image, under which he continuously dwelt. So that, when we think of him, we uniformly think of eminent spirituality, and of loftiest purity. We think of Peter the impetuous, of Paul the learned, of Apollos the orator, but of

John the *saint*. An air of sanctity pervades his name; and, in our common view, he is the brightest reflection of the Saviour's character. He was the devoutest and nearest disciple of Christ, and received most of his Master's image. He had the most intimate communion with Christ; and, as "conversation is assimilating," John received into himself most fully the mind that was in *Him*, and he became in all things conformed to the example of his Master. His temper and disposition were like Christ's. There was real congeniality, which is essential to intimate friendship. There was in John perfect love, Christian perfection, maturity in spiritual excellence.

His Epistles are so full of love, and so pure and rich in saving truths, that they might have been written by Christ Himself. How redolent they are with purity; how abhorrent they are of sin; how strongly they declare that "whosoever is born of God doth not commit sin!" How tenderly and compassionately they inculcate brotherly love; what high spirituality they breathe; what sweet fragrance of devotion, what incense of prayer and thanksgiving, perfume them! St. Jerome hands down a tradition of the earlier Fathers, that the knees of the apostle John were hard as camel's knees with prayer. John had often been with his Master apart in a desert place for devotion; he had ofttimes gone with the Saviour to the Mount of Olives for communion with the Father; and the effect of this appears in all he wrote and did.

And how calm and serene John was in *heavenly contemplation!* As he approached the close of life, he dwelt, in thought, increasingly on his Master's last address, by which the Saviour stilled the troubled hearts of His disciples with words on His Father's house of many mansions, which He was going to prepare for them. And when, in the rocky islet, John saw visions of earthquakes, and darkness, and smoke,—where horses appeared up to the very bridles in blood, and where Death on his Pale Horse rides forth stamping with iron hoofs the ground into graves; yet, amidst all this progressive ruin and desolation, the record of which has made Popes and despots writhe in their beds and tremble on their thrones, how calmly he, the child-like apostle, beholds the New Jerusalem coming down from God out of heaven, and the pure river of the water of life flowing onward from the throne, with its over-hanging trees for the healing of all nations! Spirituality and heavenly-mindedness are characteristic features of St. John. These he had learned from Christ; from the study of His spirit, and from careful conformity to His pattern in devotion, and to His example in prayer and heavenly contemplation, until he had become *Christ-like*. And pre-eminently because he was *Christ-like*, he was pre-eminently "the disciple whom Jesus loved."

It was so with the beloved disciple just departed from us. He had much of the Divine Master's lovable image and likeness. He was gentle, meek, and lowly; having learned this of Christ. Christian modesty was evident in all he did and said. There was no vaunting of himself. Loved and honoured as he was, there was no boasting of what he had been, and of what he had done. Like the holy John, who hides himself in nameless allusions, and in sweet circumlocutions, as one of the *two* disciples who were first to follow Jesus; as " that disciple whom Jesus loved;" and as " the other disciple who did outrun Peter;" so our departed friend, in real humility, in true modesty, glorified not himself. "Meek JOHN HANNAH" was the descriptive phrase given him in youth, and which belonged to him all his days. Those who knew him in this city, when a boy, will recall his modest, humble character. So gentle, so retiring; so fearful of being thought obtrusive, even from a child. When, in this dear old Lincoln, he beheld his sinfulness, and an aged leader, NOBLE SPROWLE, asked him of his state, his only answer was, " Worse and worse!" And when, at length, he found the Lord to be " merciful and gracious, pardoning iniquity, transgression, and sin,"—as an aged class-mate declared,—the grateful joy expressed was so humble, so prostrate, that the oldest believer was filled with adoring wonder before God.

His *devotional fervour* was marked by all who knew him. His worshipping spirit was awed and prostrated in the presence of Jehovah. He seemed to shrink into nothing before God. Like the angels who cover their faces with their wings in the presence of the Most High, so he, profoundly reverent, abased and hid himself, being *clothed* with humility. What awe and solemn feeling he manifested in his prayers! He truly approached the throne of grace with fear and trembling. And when, through the blood of atonement, and the mediation of Christ, he passed within the veil to the mercy-seat, how his devout soul kindled with feeling of adoration until he seemed radiant under the shining forth of the Divine glory! Who that has been with him in social, family, or public prayer does not remember this? Thoughtless, *mindless* familiarity with the dread and awful Jehovah in prayer was utterly foreign to his reverent and humble soul. His prayer was solemn, thoughtful, devout prayer, as all prayer should be. And in his kindlings into spiritual fervour, and in his pleadings with God, it was evident that his whole heart was prayerful. The very manner and language of his audible prayer proclaimed intimacy with closet-worship, and that he cherished habitual prayer of the heart. It was plain that he had often been on the mountain apart, where a bright cloud had overshadowed him. Yea, like Moses, his very face shone with the glory that rested upon him.

And so with *sweet* and *heavenly contemplation.* He was a cheerful, happy Christian, looking towards his heavenly home, and waiting until his Lord should come to receive him. Perhaps he preached as many funeral sermons for deceased Christians as any minister of our day that could be named; and they were all Christian funeral sermons, radiant with hope and joyful expectation.

So with his ministry to the church. It was heavenly in its tone and colouring; it was of " the better country;" it was on the surpassing blessedness of being with Christ, and with the white-robed company of the redeemed. Of the same holy character was his conversation; and that to the end, when he exclaimed, " All is well! I shall soon be where the weary are for ever at rest." Like his Lord, he looked to the joy set before him. And in conformity to his Master's image—in gentleness, goodness, meekness, lowliness, true spirituality, and heavenly-mindedness—he was " the disciple whom Jesus loved."

4. Once more, I observe the beloved disciple rendered FIRM AND RESOLUTE OBEDIENCE TO HIS MASTER'S COMMANDS. John was not a weak, timorous Christian, yielding to any strong influence that came upon him. He was, naturally, an impulsive and an aspiring man. He and his brother were called "Boanerges—the sons of thunder."

Through his mother, he sought the very highest place in Christ's kingdom; to sit immediately on the right or left of the Kingly Messiah. And when opposing Jews appeared before Christ, John was for calling down fire swift from heaven to destroy them. So that, naturally, John was ambitious and impetuous. But grace humbled and subdued him. The ardour of his nature was sanctified and governed by love. His chariot was yoked to fiery steeds that bore him towards the sun—that drew him straight to heaven; and he mounted, daily, higher and higher. His integrity and firmness of purpose were not abolished. They were only changed in their object and aim.

There was a *strong side* in St. John, as there is in all truly great men, however simple and modest they may be. His writings show this. Some of the strongest language is found in them; declaring that "whosoever hateth his brother is a murderer;" that "he that committeth sin is of the devil;" and that "if a man say, I love God, and hateth his brother, he is a liar." His calm survey of the visions of the Apocalypse is evidence of it; and his patient endurance of suffering "for the word of God, and for the testimony of Jesus Christ," corroborates it. To say nothing of early tradition, which reports that he indignantly refused to continue in a public bath with Cerinthus, the heretic, lest the building should fall and crush that enemy of the Lord;—or of his being cast into a caldron of boiling oil by order of Domitian, who afterwards banished him to Patmos;—and how, in old age, he braved exposure to a band of notorious robbers on the mountains, to recover from among them a prodigal convert, who had become their chief;—to say nothing of these traditionary evidences from almost apostolic times, it is evident from the Scriptures that he was firmly and perseveringly obedient. It is a false idea that calm, contemplative men are weak and infirm of purpose. The lion and the leopard are gentle in their usual movements as the lamb. The stormy sea that roars and is troubled, lifting up its waves for destruction, often rests as serenely in its bed as an infant. Deep rivers do not babble like the shallow brook. And often the strongest and most earnestly persevering men are in their ordinary manner as simple as children. They do not spend their strength in noisy professions, but in real practical service. It was so with St. John. He wavered not in his course. He never left the Saviour from the hour of his call by the Jordan. He was with Jesus daily; and to the end was a faithful and obedient disciple. He was in the judgment-hall; stood by the cross; and, firm to his purpose, he continued to tarry in suffering and obedience for seventy long years, until Christ came to receive him to Himself. He taught, and suffered, and laboured through this prolonged period, opposing error, correcting heresy, instructing and warning the church, perseveringly obedient to the commands of his Master; and was thus "the disciple whom Jesus loved."

And *decision of character*—stern, resolute, persevering obedience—marked Dr. Hannah, as much as gentleness and modesty. They who viewed him as a man void of strong feeling did not know him. His indignation at meanness, forwardness, and selfishness was powerful indeed. His rebukes for misconduct and disobedience were terrible: not in fierce, jagged words, but in solemnity of tone and earnestness. It was Love reproving. It was oil on fire. It was purity kindled against impropriety and sin. Disturbers of the church, injurious persons, never had more solemn and condemnatory remonstrances from any lips than from his. He could be angry and sin not; and, like the apostle John, he would not dwell with sinners. Dr. Hannah was no pliant weakling. He was a firm and unflinching promoter of what was right and good; and he was an open and bold denunciator of what was false and wicked. He was a resolute opponent of Popery, wherever it appeared; whether among its own professed adherents, or among those bearing the name and inheriting the immunities of Protestantism. He alike condemned ceremonial Ritualism on the one hand, and sceptical Rationalism on the other. His love to Christ, and his zeal for his Divine Lord's honour, ensured this. Fidelity to the Saviour, to whom he had devoted his mind and heart, required it; and he was resolute and determined in obedience. And in all the Divine requirements he sought to be faithful. He had "respect to all God's commandments," and that to the end of life. Who ever beheld in him anything discreditable to the religion he professed? Whenever did he, by word or deed, cause the enemy to blaspheme? Who ever suspected him of want of integrity, truth, or righteousness? Whose character was not safe in his keeping? Whose reputation suffered through him? I am not intending to utter for him unqualified praise, or to be understood as representing him as absolutely perfect, and in no respects defective. That belongs not to any mortal; and to overpraise is, practically, to detract from merit. It is to commit what has been designated among men "the unpardonable sin."

The sun has its spots, and Dr. Hannah had his defects. His guileless, unsuspecting nature, sometimes, was open to imposition; and, perhaps, he needed more of the wisdom of the serpent, associated with the harmlessness of the dove. And his extreme sensibility, and feminine tenderness, now and then exposed him to unnecessary pain and grief. Harsh, unfeeling manner, and strong words uttered in the heat of debate, wounded him; and though he might not complain, yet he would retire and brood over what had been said or done. But morally and religiously before man—while, like the best of human beings, defective and defiled before God—he was in Christian deportment and conduct "unblamable," as the Scripture terms it. As in St. John, so also in him, there was symmetry and maturity of Christian character. His obedience to the Master's commands was uniform, constant, and to the end. He was faithful unto death, and thus was "the disciple whom Jesus loved."

To trace the course of one so excellent, and to note the circumstances in which he obtained the moral likeness and distinguished love of Jesus, will now be our pleasing employment. But, before we proceed to this, it may be well for us to sing together part of the 51st hymn :—

> "Hark ! a voice divides the sky,
>   Happy are the faithful dead !
> In the Lord who sweetly die,
>   They from all their toils are freed.
> Them the Spirit hath declared
>   Blest, unutterably blest :
> Jesus is their great Reward,
>   Jesus is their endless Rest.
>
> "Follow'd by their works, they go
>   Where their Head hath gone before ;
> Reconciled by grace below,
>   Grace had open'd Mercy's door ;
> Justified through faith alone,
>   Here they knew their sins forgiven ;
> Here they laid their burden down,
>   Hallow'd and made meet for heaven."

BIOGRAPHICAL SKETCH.

---✠---

DOCTOR HANNAH was born at Lincoln, November 3, 1792, in a house situated south of the water-side, near the "Swing Bridge," where his father resided, as a maltster and corn-merchant; which house, together with adjoining premises, since improved and built upon at the formation of "Melville-street," leading from the new bridge to the Cliff-road, the son possessed and valued to the end of life, as his paternal inheritance.

His father, Mr. John Hannah, was originally from Faldingworth, in Lincolnshire, where he was born in the month of March, 1747. Afterwards he removed with his parents to Toft-Newton, in the same county, and spent there the early part of his life in husbandry with his father, who was a farmer. According to a manuscript record from the hand of the deceased, his grandparents on the father's side were strictly moral and upright in their conduct; and as soon as they had the opportunity of hearing the saving truth of the Gospel, they cordially embraced it. Their son, DR. HANNAH's father, was early the subject of religious influence. When little more than seven years of age, he heard the Rev. Thomas Hanby, an early Methodist Preacher; and was brought by what he heard nigh to the kingdom of God. When twenty years old, by the instrumentality of the Rev. John Peacock, an eminently good man, and an earnest preacher of the Gospel, he was joined to a Methodist class-meeting for Christian fellowship and counsel. And thus, under the teaching of religious experience,—the best teaching he could have,—he was impelled to seek acceptance with God through Jesus Christ, until he found it, and consciously rejoiced in the favour of the

Most High. Some years after this, DR. HANNAH's father became impressed with the necessity of baptism by immersion, and united himself with the General Baptists who worshipped behind St. Benedict's church in this city. And, in the humble burial-ground, there he and his wife, the mother of DR. HANNAH, have their last earthly resting-place.

DR. HANNAH's father ever retained a love for the Methodists, among whom he had been brought to a saving knowledge of the truth. And, on their establishment in Lincoln, he cast in his lot with them; and from thence to the end of life worshipped with them in their first chapel by the water-side, near to his residence, and availed himself of their most spiritual means and ordinances. According to his son's record of him in a paper written three weeks after the father's death, he was a plain, unpretentious man, remarkably diffident and retiring; but possessed a good understanding; and was careful to furnish his mind by diligent study of history, geography, and scriptural theology.

He was attentive to parental obligations, as also to the closet-duties of religion; and regularly read the Scriptures and prayed in his family twice on each day, seeking to train up his children in the way in which they should go. He increasingly matured in Christian character until November 3, 1817, when, somewhat suddenly, but smiling with joyous hope, he passed to his eternal rest.

Dr. Hannah's mother was not the first wife of his father. Her name was Elizabeth Young; and after her marriage with Mr. John Hannah she became his cheerful and devout associate, both in personal and domestic piety. She died early, about the year 1798 or 9, according to the crumbling record on the family grave-stones, in the old Baptist burial-ground, where she is described as John Hannah's second wife. From the old Bible-Registry it appears that by this second marriage there were five children, among whom Dr. Hannah was one of the youngest.

Thus Dr. Hannah's early childhood and youth were spent under the immediate influence of godly example and scriptural instruction; and when very young the fear of God was strong within him. Some youthful acts of disobedience are related of him; such as stealing out of chapel, after he had heard the text, so as to be able to repeat it at home when he should be asked to do so,—and then, with Sabbath-breaking boys, repairing to his father's garden, climbing an apple-tree for fruit, and breaking his wrist by a heavy fall to the ground. But, generally speaking, his youth was marked by dutiful obedience to his parents, and by strict propriety of conduct. Like his father, he was exceedingly shy and retiring. He shunned company, rather than sought it; and in his boyhood he was noted for thoughtful and studious habits. To be fully out of view, he would climb up into a thickly-shaded tree with his book, and read it uninterruptedly, astride on one of its stronger boughs, and under its over-hanging branches; or, he would leave his bed before sunrise, walk over the fields and the "Common" to

Canwick, that before the world was astir he might have full and free scope for thought and reflection.

He was evidently a favourite with his step-mother, who supplied him with money for the purchase of books. It is said that the Rev. Daniel Isaac was his first schoolmaster; but that fear of Mr. Isaac's severity induced his father to remove John early to another for instruction. The family relate that a Mr. Andrewes was his first schoolmaster; and that afterwards, for education, he was with Mr. Bainbridge, and then with the Rev. Mr. Gray, one of the vicars of the Cathedral. At first he was slow to learn, notwithstanding his strong desire for knowledge: but afterwards he made rapid progress; so that his clerical instructor, who was one of the best classical scholars in the county, declared that he was his first pupil in English and Greek. His grounding in English, Hebrew, and the classic languages was thorough; and his mind was disciplined by early study of mathematics. In manhood he was diligent in building upon these firm foundations; so that he became a really good and highly-accomplished scholar, worthy of the designation of "a learned man." To his latest years he retained the habit of early rising for study; and to the end of his days he was diligently adding to his stores of various knowledge; so that his mind was filled with the most valuable information, which he copiously poured forth for the interest and profit of others.

The particular circumstances belonging to his *conversion* to God are not known. He was not accustomed, in the modesty of his nature, to speak of himself; and others are not able now to mark the several steps which led to this all-important change. His case was one of gradual and increasing illumination by the Holy Spirit. He was not suddenly brought out of darkness into light. From his youth up he feared the Lord; and though there was with him, as in all who are born of God, a distinct moment when he passed from death unto life, yet, under the increasing impartation of Divine teaching and influence, the instant of time when he was "born again" was not in his case so apparent as in some others. But when by the "assurance of faith," and the "witness of the Spirit," he knew that he had found acceptance, and been made, for Christ's sake, a child of God, he rejoiced with the humble and adoring joy already described. This was at the age of seventeen years. The inspired description of the youth of Samuel seems to be beautifully applicable to him: "The child grew on, and was in favour both with the Lord, and also with men." (1 Sam. ii. 26.) The knowledge of his own case, as well as that of his father, made him specially careful through life not to limit the Holy Spirit's modes of operation in conversion. While emphatically and unmistakably insisting on an inward and spiritual change, which must have its decisive time of occurrence, yet he did not teach or require that in *all* cases, without exception, the precise moment of that change must necessarily be known by him who experiences it. He deemed it sufficient, in these cases of gradual enlightenment and of Divine drawings, that it be known by the Spirit's testimony within, and by the Spirit's fruits without, that the great change has been accomplished.

For securing growth in grace, DR. HANNAH attentively sought the aid of religious means and ordinances. He daily searched the Scriptures that he might become wise unto salvation. He prayed in the family; though at first, in his diffidence, he imposed the condition that, in doing so, he should kneel apart in an adjoining room, from which, unseen by him, they could hear his voice. He often entered into his closet, shut the door, and prayed to his Father who seeth in secret, and rewardeth openly. He regularly attended public worship, and eagerly drank in the sincere milk of the word. He weekly met with them "that feared the Lord, spake often one to another, and that thought upon His name." In 1809 he was a member of old Mr. Brumby's class, which met in his father's house, and which formerly was led by Mr. Smith. And when, afterwards, Mr. Bainbridge became a class-leader, Dr. HANNAH associated himself with his early friend and adviser, and his name was enrolled second in Mr. Bainbridge's class-list. To secure more intimate Christian communion on the dealings of God with the souls of His people, he met in weekly private band, on Sunday morning at six o'clock, before attending the prayer-meeting at seven, with Mr. William Bacon, afterwards in the Methodist ministry, and Mr. William Parker, afterwards his brother-in-law. Spiritual self-culture was what he sought earnestly and diligently; and his object was successfully realized. His profiting appeared to all.

His first attempt at *preaching* was in a cottage occupied jointly by a blind woman named Mrs. Harrison, and a Miss, or, as she was called, Mrs. Crofts, at the village of Waddington, some five miles south of Lincoln, where at that time the Rev. Richard Waldo Sibthorpe wrought assiduously as the parish curate, and who not unfrequently seated himself on a stool in this cottage, and conversed with these aged Christians on experimental religion. Previously to this, young John Hannah endeavoured to do good as he had opportunity. He had engaged publicly in prayer, though with manifest fear and trembling; he had visited the sick and the poor; and in a small room which he hired by the water-side, near to the Magpies' Inn, he had opened a Sunday-school in Lincoln, where Mrs. Flint and others, at his solicitation, became teachers, and which prospered greatly. This was before the "Bank's Sunday-school," afterwards built by him on his own ground; and was the first Sunday-school in Lincoln. But his friends, believing that he was intended for a wider sphere of usefulness, urged him to commence preaching. Mr. William Mawer, and Messrs. Bacon and Parker, his band-companions, especially besought him to make the attempt; and, at length, accompanied by Mr. Parker, he undertook this cottage-service among a few simple-minded villagers. His text on the occasion was from 2 Cor. viii. 9: "For ye know the grace of our Lord Jesus Christ, that, though He was rich, yet for your sakes He became poor, that ye through His poverty might be rich." His diffidence at the beginning almost overcame him. To use his own expression of feeling, he "thought the effort would have killed him;" but he grew increasingly confident as he proceeded; and, as he stated to the students in the dining-hall at Didsbury shortly before his death, when referring to his first sermon, in its evangelical character, he then "struck the key-note of his preaching for life." He was at that time nineteen years of age.

Soon after this, at the urgent request of the Rev. John Draper, the minister then stationed in Lincoln, and on the stipulated condition that it should not be previously made known, he preached in the city chapel by the water-side, from Luke xi. 13: "If ye then, being evil, know how to give good gifts unto your children: how much more shall your heavenly Father give the Holy Spirit to them that ask Him?" This was on a Wednesday evening, in 1812. The impression produced by his sermon, both upon minister and people, was, that he was intended by the Head of the church for the Christian ministry. Indeed, though backward to speak of this to others, and reluctant to attempt preaching, yet, incidentally, it was shown that he had an abiding impression on his own mind that he was designed by God to go forth into the world and preach the Gospel. He was stimulated to study by this impression. With it, he reluctantly engaged in any earthly pursuits. His father had hoped to have in him a helper and successor in business; but had to relinquish this cherished hope, and to yield to the entreaty of the son, that he might have opportunity and means for entire devotion to learning.

On one occasion, when having been much longer in the performance of some assigned service than necessary, his father inquired,

"John, has this work taken you all this time?" "No, father," was the son's reply. "Then what have you been doing besides?" was asked. "I have been preaching, father," was the answer. "How preaching?" rejoined the disconcerted sire: "you could have no congregation where you were, but cocks and hens!" On another occasion, when undertaking to grind malt, he was found bathed in perspiration, and continuing to turn over the handle long after all the malt put into the funnel had been crushed. His father, entering the maltkiln, and seeing how things were, exclaimed, "John, what are you doing? you are distressing yourself; and there has been no malt to grind for some time." "I was preaching my trial-sermon before the Methodist Conference," was the answer. And his preaching in the towns and villages of the Lincoln Circuit, which at that time also included the places since separated for the Sleaford Circuit, was highly acceptable. So, by the counsel of the Circuit-ministers, and of highly-valued friends, then influential Methodists in the city,—such as Mr. William Mawer, Mr. Thomas Bainbridge, Mr. Brumby, Mr. W. S. Parker, and others, —he was nominated by the superintendent-minister of the Lincoln Circuit for the Methodist ministry, and was cordially recommended to the Conference for that spiritual office by the Quarterly and District Meetings.

It must have been during the interval between his recommendation for the ministry and his first appointment by the Conference, that a call seemed to be made upon him to go with Dr. Coke to India; a call which he showed himself ready to obey. The Doctor had obtained authority from the Conference to take with him seven young men as companion-missionaries to India. But fearing that some one of those selected for this service should fail him near the time of departure, he inquired who were the most devoted candidates for the ministry, in order that he might readily fill up the number that might suddenly become deficient. JOHN HANNAH was highly recommended to him as "a most excellent young man for this service" as we learn from letters of correspondence with Dr. Clarke, then President of the Conference, found among Dr. Coke's papers after his death. The Doctor wrote to the youthful candidate for the ministry, to inquire if he would be willing to accompany him as a missionary to India. JOHN HANNAH wrote to Dr. Coke the following reply, dated

"Lincoln, August 10th, 1813.

"Rev. and Dear Sir,

"I received your first letter on Sunday night, and your second last night. I rejoice to hear of your benevolent purposes towards the Indians, and think you confer great honour on me by inviting me to engage with you in so glorious an undertaking. I shall certainly feel it painful to leave my friends,—particularly my father,—and to resign all my comfortable prospects in England; yet, if I be conscious that it is the will of God, I think, with the assistance of His grace, I can make these sacrifices. The Lord Jesus was induced for my sake to lay aside the glory and felicity of heaven; and I cannot think it hard for His sake to renounce a few comforts on earth. My father consents to my going. I have consulted my friends on the subject; and they unanimously think, that if I can trust my all with God, I ought to go. The chief objection I feel to it, is my great deficiency in missionary abilities and in piety. Did I abound in these, I think I could go with pleasure. As things are, if you think proper to accept of me, I must say, though with a considerable portion of timidity, I am at your service.

"I shall be greatly obliged to you to inform me, whether those who engage in this mission engage in it for life, or not. You will, also, be so kind as to mention the time when you intend to sail; the conveniences and inconveniences attending the voyage; the preparations that are requisite on my part; with everything else that you think it necessary for me to know, in order to form a clear and distinct conception of the intended mission.

"The thought of going under your direction, and your kind promise of being a father to me, strongly incline me to comply with your request.

"Praying that God may crown your design with His approbation, and make the mission abundantly successful in diffusing the light of the Gospel among the benighted Indians,

"I remain, Rev. and Dear Sir,

"Your unworthy servant in the Gospel,

"JOHN HANNAH."

This prudential arrangement by Dr. Coke

was not carried out, no failure among the missionaries engaged requiring it. But JOHN HANNAH's letter proves that, at any cost of home-comforts, family-ties, discomforts and dangers of the voyage, and service abroad for life, if required, he was prepared for Christ's sake to go a missionary to India. And in all after-life—though he made no boast of it, and scarcely named it—it was a circumstance of grateful remembrance by him that, by Divine grace, he had been enabled to sacrifice all personal considerations, and to offer himself without reserve for the service and glory of Christ.

His first appointment by the Conference was to the Bruton Circuit, in Somersetshire, in the year 1814; his next to the Gainsborough Circuit, in his own county; his next to Bridlington, in Yorkshire; and his next to Lincoln, the Circuit which bore the name of his native city. In these Circuits he ministered acceptably and usefully; and from a letter sent from his first Circuit to his friend Mr. Bainbridge, dated March 4, 1815, it is evident that from the beginning he diligently applied himself to improve the advantages of his classical and mathematical education, and to become "a scribe well instructed for the kingdom of God." In this letter he says,—after referring to his general studies, and reading of the best authors,—"I am seeking to get clearer views of Theology, which is my first business." The Lincoln Circuit was then, as now, somewhat extensive in territory, and included numerous villages in its compass. He walked and rode cheerfully to the villages and hamlets belonging to it, carrying with him books in his pockets, or in his saddle-bags; and interesting incidents are related of him in those times. One is, that an aged Christian woman near Saxilby awoke very early one morning, and told her husband that she must rise, make a fire, and heat the kettle; for the impression on her mind that she should do so was so strong that it seemed as if a voice spoke to her. The husband sought to persuade her that it was only a dream. She found, however, that she could not rest, and so arose, made a fire, and boiled the kettle. When she had done so, she looked out at the door, saw some person coming by the side of the river, who, as he approached, showed himself to be her minister, Mr. Hannah. She inquired how it was that he was abroad so early. He replied, that, being unwell, he was desirous of going home; and not wishing to awake the family at whose house he had passed the night, he had left them without making it known that he did so; but that he was now faint, and ready to fall. The good old woman said to him, "Come in, and have some tea; for I now see why I had to rise, and get it ready." He did so, and then walked briskly home.

Those of the Lincoln Circuit now living will remember the deep interest attending his ministry here. The evangelical character of his preaching,—its fervent, glowing style,—and, above all, the Divine unction which attended it, cannot be forgotten. His deep humility and constitutional diffidence often depressed him; so that, after the delivery of the most edifying discourse, he was afraid to meet his hearers in the chapel-ground; and, to escape from doing so, was known to lock himself up in the vestry until all had gone, and he could pass unobserved to his home. But his edifying and powerful sermons did much to quicken and elevate Methodism in Lincoln, and in the surrounding neighbourhood. Persons of education and of considerable *status* in society were attracted by his public ministry to the chapel at St. Swithin's. "The common people heard him gladly." And his loving, catholic spirit—shown to all followers of Christ, of every name, at meetings for the Bible Society and other public institutions—brought Wesleyans into glad and happy association with pious, evangelical clergymen, and devout Nonconformists of different denominations. Those were days when the good of surrounding churches were fewer, and more marked in their distinctive character; —days when, notwithstanding the flagrant immorality evinced by some even high in the ministerial office, and the more open derision poured upon devoted followers of the Saviour, real spiritual sympathy and essential union were manifested by those of the several churches who had separated themselves in spirit, as well as in profession, to live godly in Christ Jesus. The ministry of DR. HANNAH—as did also the ministry of the Revs. Daniel Isaac, Thomas Galland, and John Smith—gave, under God, successive impulses to Methodism in Lincoln, that demonstrably raised it in numerical importance and also in social consideration and position. Citizens of all classes thronged to hear these preachers, and also crowded the chapel when eminent ministers—such as Clarke, Bunting, Watson, Lessey, and Newton—officiated in it, for Missions, and other institutions of the Connexion.

DR. HANNAH married August 12, 1817, at St. Swithin's church in this city, Miss Jane Caparn, the sister-in-law of his friend and bandmate, Mr. W. S. Parker, already named; and found in her a devoted wife, fully suited to him in intelligence, goodness, and large-hearted sympathy with his views and cares.

This "elect lady," loved and revered by all who have known her, during the extended period of fifty years, was to her husband a true "help meet," sustaining and encouraging him in all his important and responsible services; and she, "the wife of his youth," lived to the end of his days, gratefully in his very "heart of hearts," as his dearest earthly treasure. It was truly beautiful to witness in ripe old age his devoted affection for his wife. Reverence for woman was strong in him, as it is in every manly spirit; but his "dear Jane," painfully afflicted of late years, had daily his first and most ardent attention. When from home, post-letters by the morning's delivery were eagerly seized by him, that he might read first his suffering wife's epistle; and afterwards, before anything else was done, he would write to his beloved one in terms glowing with the enflamed ardour of pure and matured affection. And when public services or friendly visitations no longer detained him, he expressed exultantly the joyous anticipation he cherished of returning to Mrs. Hannah. It was ever so with him; and not the less so on his last return to her, which was from my house in London, only a few days before he died.

After remaining three years a minister in Lincoln, he was stationed successively, for three years in each place, at Nottingham, Leeds, Manchester, and Huddersfield; by which he became more publicly known, and more generally appreciated. The rich savour of his godly character, and the Divine unction which signally attended his ministration, made him eminent; and in all those towns and their surrounding districts he became precious and beloved. His preaching was expository and practical: it was not argumentative. The mind of the Spirit as expressed in the Scriptures was diligently sought for by prayerful study, and then explicitly given. It was not florid and highly-elaborated. Truth, in his view, was not many-coloured, but clear and transparent as the purest crystal. Hence, he set it forth in its own beauty, and not with tinselled adornment and cloying imagery. His style was remarkably pure and simple; and his preaching had an evident directness of aim that none could misunderstand. The truth was faithfully apportioned and applied to his hearers, according to their respective characters; and the whole was earnestly delivered with the kindled fervour of sincere earnestness, and with yearning compassion over sinners whom he sought to save from impending destruction.

His Sunday morning and week-day evening sermons were almost uniformly addressed to the members of the church, and were most instructive and spiritually refreshing. His Sunday evening sermons had, usually, a direct bearing upon the state of the unconverted, and were most searching and powerful. He was not what would be termed, at least in this sensational age, a "striking preacher." He was too well-balanced in his powers, and too profoundly reverent, as well as too symmetrical in his carefully-cultivated mind, to utter startling extravagances, that might be deemed by superficial thinkers "original" and "effective." His imagination was quick and lively, lighting up all he said. Much of poetic feeling was in him, giving vividness, tone, and colouring to his style; but all was chastened, and subdued into rich mellowness, by due sense of proportion and propriety. Hence, all he did had a character of completeness, and was never wearisome by being extravagantly extended. It was said and done within the time allotted—and done well; so that all who heard him would be ready to exclaim, "True and admirable!" But for wonder-loving seekers of novelty and eccentricities, his preaching had not the attractive qualities they desire. Nor was his manner of delivery, according to the rules of elocutionists and position-masters, commendable. His inobtrusive timidity and natural modesty made him restless and uneasy in physical attitude and motions; and in the earlier part of his ministry, especially, he was rapid and outgushing in his pulpit-utterances. But his friends and all who lovingly remember him would not have changed his manner, if they could have done so. While unsuitable as models, his manner, gesture, style, and delivery were parts of himself, and were in good keeping with his own thoughts and feelings.

He was, however, in the only valuable sense of the phrase, "a popular preacher;" and that not merely for a brief shining period of youthful ardour, but during the fifty-three years of his ministerial life. He had not to console himself—as some inanimate self-complacent preachers do—that he had the "discerning few" to hear him. He had, throughout his course, large and attentive congregations, composed of all classes. The more thoughtful, and best educated, found in his discourses scholarly and manly dealing with the truth. He indulged in no vague and cloudy speculations, such as sometimes give, by mystic, visionary forms, false reputation for "sublimity." He shirked no difficulty in the interpretation of the word of God. But the truth as revealed, and as understood by proper rendering, and by sincere, unbiassed minds, he proclaimed plainly and openly. And his abiding sense of the high responsibility of his office, as an ambassador for Christ,—sent to beseech men in the Saviour's stead to be reconciled to God,—kindled into high fervour the strong feelings of his nature, and made him, under the unction of the Spirit, lively, energetic, and powerful. His calls to sinners to repent and live—after the text had been expounded—were sometimes at the full extent of his voice, so that the assembly was thrilled with emotion under his beseeching cries. "Bless ye," said a plain man at Stockport to his fellow-worshippers, on hearing him in the last year of his life, "this old man has more fire in him than ten of the younger preachers put together that come to us in these days." The ardour of his preaching never lost its glow. It might not in maturer and later years break forth at points into as brilliant coruscations as it did in his youth; but it burned to the very end, and that, if with a steadier, yet with a stronger flame. He was, as a preacher, as well as in his Christian character, "a burning and a shining light," which searched the heart and conscience, as well as illumined the understanding.

The *devotional services* of the sanctuary were conducted by him with the strictest order and propriety. He loved the service of sacred song, and most reverently and adoringly engaged in it. His public prayers were tremblingly devout. A solemn sense of Divine majesty was upon him, when he approached the throne of grace, and led the supplications of the congregations. Humility and profound self-abasement were evident in his confessions of sin. Reliance upon Christ's atoning sacrifice and mediatorial intercession was manifest in his pleadings for mercy. Knowledge of human life and character, in its varieties of temptation, anxiety, and suffering, was shown in his petitions for growth in grace, and for seasonable strength and consolation. Love of his nation, loyalty to his sovereign and government, concern for all classes of the community, and compassionate interest in distant tribes and nations of heathen and idolatrous men, were expressed and made known in his public prayers, as well as his earnest desire for the immediate awakening and conversion of the unregenerate around him. And there were times, memorable with many who were privileged to worship with him in public, when he seemed to reach the very mercy-seat, and to be adoring and pleading amidst the beaming glory of the Divine presence, under the outstretched wings of the cherubim; as there were also times in his preaching when his face seemed to shine with the radiance of the bright cloud which overshadowed him. His reading of the word of God was deliberate and emphatic. He read it with the reverence due to its Author, and not as a mere "lesson" that had to be gone through. And at the end of the service he reserved time for praying over the principal truths set forth in his sermon; seeking with the devout of the congregation, who "helped him together with their prayers," that the Holy Spirit would apply and render effectual the word that had been preached. Devotion, indeed, was the element of his being. He lived and moved in it. He never trifled with spiritual things, nor could others do so in his presence. "Thou God seest me" seemed to be written upon his heart; and in public worship, as in private life, he was always reverent and devout.

In *social gatherings* of the members of the churches, and on the *platform* at public meetings, Dr. Hannah often appeared. Notwithstanding his natural diffidence and retiring modesty, he was truly sociable in his character. He was no stern ascetic, shrinking from society, as if it could not be touched without contamination. He was a cheerful, loving Christian, who enjoyed the company of his fellow-Christians; and he was too earnest in his desire for the extension of the Saviour's kingdom, both at home and abroad, to be unwilling to take part in its advocacy. Few men, in charge of a special department of the work of God, appeared so frequently in public to plead for the various institutions of the church.

Foreign and Home Missions, the erection of chapels, education in Sunday and Week-day schools, and charitable agencies for the sick and the poor,—all had, in turn, his ready and cheerful aid. And, whether for preaching or social and platform speaking, he would go where help was needed, whatever the character and position of the place. The humblest village or hamlet, equally with the town or metropolis, shared his presence and service. He had no great spasmodic efforts, that for appreciable return must have immense crowds as witnesses of the wonder. He loved village-preaching. He remembered his agricultural ancestry, and his cottage-services in Lincolnshire; and he was a real admirer of country scenery and life;—while his just appreciation of the relative importance of large towns and cities secured his interest in them; and the love of Christ "constrained him" in all instances. Exeter-Hall had him often at its Missionary Anniversaries; but country towns and villages had him oftener.

His speeches, like his sermons, were remarkably thorough and complete. Neither in the pulpit nor on the platform was he a *memoriter* speaker. To him, *memoriter* delivery of previously prepared composition would have been mental bondage not to be borne. He knew, also, that such exercises train the mind unequally, and employ its powers unhealthily,—straining the memory beyond proportionate use, and leaving other important faculties comparatively unemployed; so that, as years advance, the mind weakens and becomes increasingly disposed to rest upon early compositions, without giving out, as it ought, the accumulations of knowledge and experience. He knew the necessity and value of written composition for forming the style in public speaking; and in earlier life he had paid careful attention to this. But he held, and said truly, that the finished style of written composition is not the natural nor most effective style of preaching or public speaking; that a more homely, free, and more direct style of address belongs both to the pulpit and to the platform, than to the written composition,—a style that leaves the preacher and speaker at liberty to interject explanations, illustrations, and observations, as they may occur to him at the time. Preparation by stored information, not from mere book-reading, but from truths and facts, however obtained, well thought out, and by arrangement of order and connection in which to be presented, is far preferable—DR. HANNAH thought—to written words which have to be exactly repeated. The embodiment and dress of spontaneous language will be— he believed—more fresh and effective than formal, stereotyped terms, however well-chosen and nicely-balanced; that what seems lost of verbal accuracy by free delivery, will be more than compensated for, in terse and effective power; and that the best preparation for preaching and public speaking consists in the solid and complete marshalling of thoughts, rather than in the mere arrangement of words.

This was DR. HANNAH's mode of preparation. His sermons were carefully written out in their plan and several divisions; having the principal facts and observations to be made briefly noted in their intended connections; but the clothing of thought, and the form of observation, were, for the most part, left to spontaneous effort at the time of delivery. And this gave continuous freshness and increasing serviceableness to his sermons and public addresses as he advanced in life. He did not simply repeat in old age what he had learned in youth. He gave to his hearers the increase which he had obtained by reading, observation, reflection, and experience. Hence, the trial-sermon which he preached more than fifty years before in the old chapel by the water-side at Lincoln, in its general arrangement and matter, was the same which he preached in City-road chapel, on the last metropolitan anniversary for Missions which he attended; but the filling up and the practical observations were added on the occasion.

Addresses and speeches he did not prepare

in writing. He pondered principal topics in his well-disciplined mind. He was not a "book-worm;" and though a diligent, yet he was not a voracious reader, filling his mental capacity with the lumber of other men's thoughts and reflections, until it could not move or exercise itself freely. His memory, like that of most great and learned men, was exact and tenacious; and his avowed purpose was to know thoroughly what he learned, or professed to receive. With this purpose, he was a man of reflection, rather than of hard reading. And when he had viewed any subject in itself, and in its different bearings and connections, and revolved it in his mind, he could produce it at will, and clothe and adorn it as he would. Hence, he was one of the most ready and most effective speakers that could be heard. He never refused to speak in public on the ground that he was not *prepared* to do so. His resources were always at command. Nor did he ever complain that they who had spoken before had taken away *his* speech. He was a generous associate in public speaking. He did not seek to outshine others, or complain of his position in the meeting. Much less did he meanly endeavour to depreciate what others had said, that he might appear the abler man. He was too noble in spirit for that. He ever remembered the apostolic injunction, "In honour preferring one another;" and he was always ready to hail a successful labourer, and to rejoice in his acceptance and success.

I have been associated with him in almost every variety of public service; and, in our intimacy, we opened, unreservedly, our private manuscripts to each other; and my deliberate and confident conclusion is, that Dr. Hannah was the most eloquent and finished extemporaneous speaker that I have known. I have not only heard him speak in social meetings, when unexpectedly called upon to do so; or in Preparatory Committee meetings, on topics of a resolution just handed to him; but I have been with him in large, influential, and representative meetings, where a visitor had to speak for a full hour on subjects, and addresses presented, which had not been so much as named until there introduced, or read;—and I never knew him at fault on his subject, break a figure or image, or trip in his sentences. Like himself, and like all he did, there was completeness and brightness in his speeches. He spoke freely and unostentatiously, out of a full heart and mind, swayed by love to God and love to man; and he was always lively and powerful. Some of his most admired deliverances, on the most delicate and solemn occasions,—such as addresses in funeral services for eminent ministers deceased,—were strictly spontaneous and unpremeditated in form. I had full means of knowing this, and in more than one instance. And so in other cases that might be specified, for public speaking Dr. Hannah was a highly-gifted and eminently-endowed servant of the Lord; and though naturally timid and retiring in himself, so as to constrain him in manner, yet—confident in God and sure of the truth—he declared boldly what he had to proclaim, both in public speaking and in preaching.

For *literary service* he was well qualified, if he could have pursued it. His Lives of the Revs. David Stoner and Theophilus Lessey; his Letter to a Junior Minister; his Inaugural Address at Didsbury; his beautiful Essay on "The Sabbath a Happy Day," included in a volume of Essays on the Christian Sabbath published in Scotland; and also the several Memoirs and Sermons published in the Wesleyan Magazine or separately,—show what he could have done if he had been favoured with "learned leisure." But the incessant hard work of Methodism does not allow this indulgence to its ministers; and it is only by snatches of time, in the midst of other pressing service, that they can prepare anything for the press.

It will readily be supposed that one so good, so gifted, so well furnished, and so " apt to teach," would be selected by his brethren for *special service* and for *honourable position*. Hence, when the time had arrived spoken of by Wesley in his earliest Conferences, by formally asking, "When shall we have a seminary for labourers?"—to which he replied, in his own characteristic style of terse, sententious brevity, "When God gives us a Tutor;" and a Theological Institution was resolved upon,—Dr. HANNAH was at once, and without dissentient opinion, chosen to be the Theological Tutor. This was in 1834, when he was removed from Liverpool North Circuit to London, that he might take this important office. The Institution was commenced in an unpretentious manner. The name of "College" was not taken for it. For not only was there prejudice by some against it, through fear of learned exaltation and trained formality; but it was evident that in the circumstances and arrangements of Methodism,—in its supply and employment of its agency,—full collegiate education and training could not be given to its accepted candidates for the ministry. A plain, humble building was hired at Hoxton, which had been used by the Congregationalists for the education of their students; and while the old dilapidated buildings were put into tenantable repair, the students were met by DR. HANNAH in the room adjoining City-road chapel. Afterwards, when full preparations had been made, the students were lodged at Hoxton, under the venerable and fatherly Joseph Entwisle, and with an efficient English and Classical Tutor. DR. HANNAH there commenced his regular course of lectures, advising on his subjects and plan with his friend and neighbour, Dr. Bunting, the President of the Institution; for whose signal ability, seasonable counsels, and disinterested services he cherished to the end of life admiring and grateful remembrances. The first company of students received for preparatory education and training were, on the whole, of superior mental capacity, and truly stimulative and encouraging to their instructors.

Afterwards, until the new Institution-buildings were provided at Richmond and Didsbury, the students were accommodated at Abney-House, Stoke-Newington; and there, for the time, Dr. Hannah gave to them theological instruction: his friend and colleague, the Rev. John Farrar, being Governor and Classical Tutor.

The *principles* held by him and its founders, for the government and objects of the Theological Institution, may be best learned from his own Inaugural Address, delivered in the college-chapel at Didsbury on the opening of the session after the Conference of 1860. They are declared therein to be, first, to nurture and promote the Students' personal Christianity; second, to lead their minds to a fuller apprehension of the grand system of Christianity in its several parts, and in its own entire harmony; third, to supply aids in literature and science, as far as time and opportunity allow, for the more successful investigation of Scriptural Truth; and, fourth, to encourage and guide the Students' practical services. These principles he acted upon, and these objects he pursued, with eminent ability, resolute fidelity, and persevering zeal. Having been appointed to this service, he resolved, in dependence upon Divine strength, to perform it to the utmost of his ability. A letter written by him to a friend at Lincoln, (Mr. Bainbridge,) just after he had been appointed to the office of Theological Tutor by the Conference of 1834, shows the spirit in which he entered upon his duties. In it he observes: "So now I start life anew. My appointment to the office which you mention was to me an object of painful apprehension, rather than of desire. It has, however, taken place. I could easily indulge in melancholy reflections on my own unfitness and incompetency; but what would these avail? An important object is set before me. I have an opportunity of rendering some assistance to those who shall bear the torch of evangelical light and salvation into distant parts of our dark world. A truce to unavailing regrets and fears! I will trust in God. I will go forth in His name and strength to this new enterprise. Appalling suggestions may be uttered; they have been uttered. I heed them not. Without any contrivance or seeking of my own, I am called by an authority which claims my obedience to essay this service. I will essay it; and if I fail, it shall not be in flight, but in effort—how feeble and ineffective soever it may prove—for the honour and glory of our Saviour." (Dated August 26, 1834.)

How he prosecuted his duties, and how he succeeded in the attainment of his objects, needs no recital. Having drawn out his scheme for lectures,—to comprehend the Evidences, the Doctrines, the Duties, and the Institutions of Christianity,—he delivered them in their course to the students committed to him for instruction, according to their respective years: not in a cold, professional manner; but with all the animation and fervour, and with all the directness of aim and application, which characterized his preaching. Filling up the prepared outline from his affluent resources as he went along, he kindled into heated fervour that awakened respondent feeling in the students before him; so that the theological lectures delivered by Dr. Hannah became means of spiritual grace to himself and to them that heard him. The power of Christianity, as well as its truth and harmony, was thus realized; and those whom he addressed were made to feel as they hearkened to him, that experimental godliness was supremely important. This, no doubt, was a main reason of the strong and universal attachment to him, personally, by the students who had been associated with him. In addition to his gentle goodness, which could not fail to win affection, it was evident that he felt deep personal interest in the students individually. He perseveringly sought their welfare and advancement, both in religious character and qualifications for usefulness. Faithful to rebuke *uppishness* and shallow pretensions, and to express the strongest indignation at unbecoming conduct, yet he was ever ready to acknowledge real merit where it appeared, and to encourage all who sought to improve their time and opportunities in preparing for the ministry.

Loving them for Christ's sake, and for the sacred work to which they were designated, he was beloved in return with filial, reverent, and enduring affection. He served in this important office thirty-three years; being eight years Theological Tutor at Hoxton and at Stoke-Newington, and twenty-five years at Didsbury, from the opening of the Northern Branch there in 1842.

' Both in the time of his work as a Circuit-minister, and during his employment as Theological Tutor, he suffered painfully through afflictions and bereavements in his family. Of eight children born to him, seven were removed by death; and one, especially, under the most sad and trying circumstances,— through a fall down stairs. Stroke after stroke fell upon him in his earthly pilgrimage, wounding him to the quick as a man and a father, until he had to exclaim, "Have pity upon me, O my friends; for the hand of the Lord hath touched me." At the loss of the seventh—that of his son Richard Watson, a most promising youth in his thirteenth year, who died of fever—he wrote a most touching letter to the Rev. Lancelot Sharpe, master of St. Saviour's School, who had taken pleasure in observing the progress of the youth while under his care; and who at his death wrote a letter of sympathy and condolence to the bereaved parents. In acknowledging this letter, Dr. HANNAH, at the close of his reply, says: "I cannot ever forget what I owe to you in behalf of my children. But I have no more whom I may have the happiness of placing under your care. Poor Richard! he is the seventh child that has, in God's merciful chastisement, been taken from us; and there is but one left. May it please God to preserve and bless him!"

But, though smitten thus severely, he did not complain, as the extract just given shows. And in his own handwriting is the proof, if it were needed, that under this heavy dispensation he bowed submissively to the Divine will. The writing is as follows, with its heading:—

"A FATHER'S PRAYER OF SURRENDER.

"May Almighty God, the great Father of the whole human family, Who has confided to us the care of this dear child for a season, and Who now calls him from us, receive him in mercy to Himself, and bless him with His own eternal presence, through Jesus Christ our Lord. Amen."

When he suffered this deep bereavement, and wrote the above, he resided at No. 8, Myddelton-square, now occupied by Rev. Dr. Hoole, senior secretary for our Missionary Society, in a house precious to Methodism; for in it resided, successively, Dr. Townley and Dr. Bunting; and in it the Rev. Richard Watson passed from earth to heaven.

Chastened and sorrowful, he held on his way as theological instructor; and the effect of his services in this office upon the Methodist ministry cannot be over-estimated. Considering not only that he was the first Theological Tutor, and shaped the course, generally, of those who shall follow him,—showing to them, and to the Methodist community, what may be done by judicious and faithful service to prepare accepted candidates for our ministry; considering, also, that a full generation of not less than four hundred ministers received their theological education and training from him; how extensively important have been the results of his labours! Imagine what different results would have appeared, if he had been uncertain in doctrine, and less watchful over the spirit and conduct of the four hundred ministers of Methodism directly instructed and influenced by him. Think how students immediately from him have gone forth to preach the word, and to feed and govern the church of God, not only in our Circuits at home, but into distant parts of the habitable globe. Methodism begun and carried on for more than thirty years past in all quarters of the globe, and almost among all nations of the earth, has, to a large extent, its type and mould from the paternal impress of DR. HANNAH's instruction and training. And that is, as all will be ready to admit, the genuine Wesleyan type. That character it will bear, unless it yields to innovation and change that shall corrupt and deteriorate it. But, wherever begun and nurtured, whether in India, Africa, or the South Sea Islands, it has had in its youth the face and form of scriptural Christianity. The effects of this must run on in successive periods, and will only be known in their finality and completeness at the last day.

So fully was Dr. Hannah viewed as a true representative man of Methodism, that he was appointed twice by his brethren to attend the General Conferences, and to visit fraternally the churches, of the "Methodist Episcopal Church of the United States of America." His first appointment was to accompany the venerable Richard Reece, in 1824; and the second, as the British Conference's Representative, in 1856. His first visit to America was attended with some personal discomfort and trouble; having left at home an afflicted child, which had been gradually sinking for months, and which died during his absence. But his personal demeanour, his fraternal addresses, and rich evangelical ministry, were highly appreciated by Methodists on the other side of the Atlantic; and, as an expression of that appreciation, they conferred upon him from their representative College, the honorary degree of Doctor in Divinity, which, coming as a courteous acknowledgment of public services, he gracefully accepted and honourably retained.

It was my privilege to accompany him on his second visit to America in 1856; and to learn, as I companioned with him day by day and night by night for nearly three months, more of his personal excellence, and eminent attainments and ability, than I had known before. As an intimate friend and a fellow-citizen, often in association and communion with him in social life and in ministerial work at home, I had previously found much to admire and love in him; but in continuous life and service together for an extended period, in ever-varying scenes and circumstances, I beheld him in the minuter details, as well as in the manly greatness, of his character. My own hopes of additional companionship had been broken; and domestic affliction, and bereavement of an intimate friend, coming suddenly, and near the time of embarking for what seemed *then* a long voyage, saddened me and made me sorrowful. The deep tenderness of his sympathizing nature was at once shown. As soon as we got out to the solitary sea, he grasped my arm, and paced the deck with me, pouring forth words of consolation. On our first night upon the deep, when the bright, piercing stars overhead cast their glancing reflections into the placid ocean, we walked step to step in the vessel, speaking of God, of His works, and of those whom we had committed, with all their anxieties and pain, to His Fatherly care. We prayed together in our cabin; unburdened ourselves to the Lord; and then, confiding in Him, sank, each down in his berth, for repose. The outpourings of his full mind and heart, during the thirteen days of our passage over the Atlantic, were wonderful. His recitals of select and appropriate pieces of poetry;

his quotations from Jeremy Taylor, Hooker, Pearson, and, above all, from the Scriptures; his references to the Wesleys, their mission to Georgia, their hymns, prose-writings, and labours; his descriptions of Boardman, Pilmoor, Asbury, Dr. Coke, and other pioneers of Methodism in America; his reminiscences of his former visit to the United States, and his expectations of what we should see, and have to do, in our mission;—all this made the days and nights spent upon the ocean with him too short; and, though some of them were fearfully tempestuous, and imminently perilous from the approximation of floating icebergs, yet one would have wished them prolonged for the intelligent and affectionate intercourse which they secured.

On landing at New York, former friends met him, and welcomed us; and as soon as "letters home" had been despatched, assuring English friends of our safe arrival in America, he was in the midst of Christian brethren and friends, pouring out his mind and heart to them. On the Sabbath morning he preached in Mulberry-street church, with the full fervour of his sanctified nature; and in the evening he attended a Missionary Meeting in the Seventh-street church, presided over by the venerable Dr. Bangs, the early historian of Methodism in the United States. After mingling some days with ministers and friends in "the great city," we proceeded by Philadelphia, Washington, Baltimore, and over the Alleghany Mountains, to Cincinnati, " the Queen city of the West," as it is termed. From thence we proceeded to Indianapolis, "the city of railroads," and the capital of the state of Indiana,—where the General Conference was to assemble,— having held the most exciting public services among both white and coloured Methodists in our way. At Indianapolis we were most cordially welcomed by the bishops, ministers, and friends, in their assembly within the State-house; and were hospitably entertained by the Governor of the State. DR. HANNAH responded heartily and affectingly to the welcome given to us; and preached and spoke energetically and eloquently at the several services and sessions we afterwards attended. His official sermon before the Conference, from 2 Cor. v. 21, "For He hath made Him to be sin for us, who knew no sin; that we might be made the righteousness of God in Him,"—afterwards supplied and published by request of the General Conference,—was richly evangelical and powerfully impressive. During its delivery there were many outbursts of "Praise the Lord!" for the "method of man's reconciliation with God" set forth in the Scriptures, and thus luminously and forcibly expounded and presented for acceptance by the British Representative. And when, after sojourning nearly three weeks among the brethren and friends at Indianapolis, we took our departure, we were thronged and followed by weeping multitudes; so greatly had DR. HANNAH, by his gentle loving spirit, and by his eloquent addresses, endeared himself to the different ranks and classes of Methodist ministers and people gathered in that city.

On leaving Indianapolis, we went further westward, to St. Louis; then up the Mississippi to Quincy; from which we crossed extended plains of rich prairie-land to Chicago, the magic city, which in forty years has advanced from a solitary hut to abodes and mansions for more than two hundred thousand inhabitants. From Chicago we went by the "lightning express" train to Detroit, where we were on the borders of the "great lakes;" and then we soon passed over Lake Erie, and by Buffalo, to the "Falls of Niagara." On gaining the Canadian side of the "Falls," where British dominion was reached, the Doctor, with all the enthusiasm of his loyal nature, lifted up his hat, waved it overhead, and shouted, "God save the Queen!" After surveying deliberately, and from its different points of view, this world of falling waters, we made our way across Lake Ontario to Toronto, where we spent several days in public services, and in fraternal intercourse with the ministers and people of Methodism in that flourishing city. Here, as in the

United States, the Doctor's presence and ministry were eagerly welcomed, and powerfully effective. After a brief sojourn here, we sped by "steamer" and "rail" to Brockville, to greet in our way the Canadian brethren, assembled in their annual Conference; and there also Dr. HANNAH spoke and preached in his own attractive and effective style. We then passed the great St. Lawrence, with its "rapids" and "thousand isles," to Montreal; and by Lake Champlain, for return to New York and England;—he turning aside for a day or two's rest with old friends at Rhinebeck, and I going eastward to see Boston, and the "Green Mountain" scenery taken on the way. In a day or two we again met; and by steamer down the romantic Hudson river returned to New York. Here we had the most friendly welcomes, and public services of affecting "farewells;" and after a good passage in our former steamer, the "Africa," reached, through Divine mercy, our own land in safety.

Thus in twelve weeks this devoted minister,

sixty-five years old, had travelled eleven thousand miles, and had engaged Sabbath after Sabbath, and week-day after week-day, in the most exciting services; and in all had not only borne up, but acquitted himself most ably. It is true, that the extreme point of effort had been reached; and both of us had to nurse ourselves in our berths by day as well as by night, on our return, for the recovery of physical and nervous vigour. But to me, in the review, it is marvellous how the "old man eloquent" should have borne that continuous strain upon his powers which he had almost perpetually to sustain on our visit to America.

In all our travels he was deeply interested in the young progressive life of the Western World. He was a devoted son of the "Old World," and venerated its constitution, and ancient laws and buildings, with enthusiasm most ardent and profound; but his mind was fully awake to the lively and promising activities of the rising States of that truly "great country." He was not the prejudiced, narrow-minded adherent to old forms that seeks to make what appropriately belongs to this "Angle-land" fit upon the vast newly-opened continents and regions of distant parts. He could appreciate the good in other lands as well as in his own. His compassionate nature showed itself, when we beheld the slave-population on the border States, and he expressed burning indignation at the recital of wrongs inflicted upon Negroes and Indians. But he was not blindly indifferent to the social and constitutional difficulties then in the way of total abolition of slavery in America; and did not sweepingly condemn all early settlers there because some of their number had wronged, and hunted down to death, the Indian aborigines. HE, whose ways are not our ways, has, by what was lawful as a war-measure, but which would have been unlawful in a time of peace, abolished the accursed evil of slavery; and where constitutional laws would not have permitted it to be done universally, and once for all, HE, the supreme Ruler of nations, has made "darkness light, and crooked things straight." And the sole glory of American emancipation of slavery belongs to HIM. DOCTOR HANNAH's thoughtful and judicious mind comprehended existing difficulties; and when they were overcome in a manner unforeseen and unthought of, gave praise to God. And in all the varying scenery of sea, rivers, city, and wilderness, beheld by us, he was the discriminating observer and the tasteful admirer. Possessed of true poetic feeling, he contemplated the beauties and wonders of creation, and the energetic activities of settled and emigrant life, with deep interest and full emotion, which evinced themselves by observations and exclamations, most instructive and appropriate.

On appearing before the Conference at Bristol, to report our reception, and deliver fraternal greetings from our brethren in America to the Methodists of great Britain, DR. HANNAH related, in his own unpremeditated and artless style, what we had seen and heard in the land, in the Conference, and among the churches to which we had been sent; and by outbursting responses, as well as by formal resolution, the ministers assembled expressed their grateful sense of the able and efficient service he had rendered on their behalf. The remembrance of this visit to America, as all his friends know, was pleasant and joyous to him.

It was not only as their representative abroad that DR. HANNAH was honoured by his brethren; but, also, in their election of him to high office at home. Nine times he was elected by them to be Secretary of the British Conference; and, though clerkship was not his *forte*, yet the many huge folio pages filled by his own handwriting in the Conference Journal show how diligently and conscientiously he performed the duties of that office. During twenty years in succession he was elected to the chairmanship of the Manchester and Bolton District; and held that responsible position with high credit to himself, and with great advantage to the Connexion. Nor during this extended period was there heard one jealous complaint from any of his brethren. Twice he was elected to be the President of the Conference,—first in London, in 1842, and afterwards in Newcastle-on-Tyne, in 1851; and on both occasions he filled that high office with acknowledged impartiality, dignity, and ability. He was, in fact, the same humble, faithful, loving servant of the Lord, whatever service he was called to perform. He did all things in the fear of God, and with love to mankind. Whether in official position in the Conference, or not, he was far from being obtrusive or forward, either in conduct or speaking. He understood well the principles and constitution of Wesleyan Methodism; and he discreetly and ably administered its laws and regulations in the several stations he held as Circuit-minister, Chairman of District, Secretary, Representative, and President of the Conference. And every agency and enterprise of the Connexion had his earnest advocacy. But he was not professedly a legislator in the church. He held in remembrance Mr. Wesley's "Rules of a Helper," in one of which it is enjoined, "Do not mend our Rules, but keep them for conscience' sake." Seldom was his voice heard in the Conference, except on direct spiritual and pastoral matters, or in defence of some essential principle. He was no coward, timid as he was naturally. Loyalty to Christ and His cause made him bold and resolute where they were assailed. But he was not a noisy advocate of unconsidered projects and questionable amendments. He recognised the original purpose of the annual assembly of Methodist ministers, to *confer* together on the work of God, and not to debate and discuss questions formally and at length, as legislative and national questions are debated and discussed in tumultuous assemblies and in the Houses of Parliament. And reverential respect for his brethren made him ever willing to hear *them*, rather than to be eager to express his own views and opinions. Where called to it, he would join in prompt, decisive, and unpopular action; but, without plain necessity for it, he shrunk from contention and the strife of tongues; and there were few things for which he had more marked contempt than for mere "talking" or "speech-making." He was in all respects *real*, and had nothing in him of the artificial.

He continued his manifold and official services until the last Conference, when, in accordance with his request, made through the District-Meeting of Manchester in May preceding, he was released from the Theological Tutorship, and was made a supernumerary minister. He was not a "worn-out" minister, but still preached and spoke with remarkable vigour and fervour. But there were times when public services produced upon him great exhaustion. Having passed more than the allotted age of threescore years and ten, the strong man began to bow himself, and public service had to be abridged and restricted. He had suffered, at periods, from rheumatic attacks; and had not unfrequently gone forth to fulfil engagements, previously made, in bodily pain and weakness that would have confined most persons to their homes, and which often ought to have confined him to his bed. On several occasions I have met him for association in public services when he was thus suffering. It was so when we met at Glossop, on Good Friday last, and when in the afternoon he preached a most pathetic and powerful sermon on the blood of Atonement. After the effort then made he had to keep his bed for several days. He found himself increasingly uncertain both for preaching and lecturing; so, with counsel and due preparation for a successor to him as Theological Tutor, he made request that he should be relieved from his office, and be allowed to become a supernumerary. Reluctant as his brethren were to comply with this request, they could not but see that it was reasonable, and that it ought to be granted.

The members of the District-Committee presented to him a most respectful and affectionate address, expressive of their sense of his personal excellence and valuable services; and of their prayerful desire that, in his comparative retirement, Divine blessing might abundantly attend him: appending the request that (if in accordance with his views and convenience) he would, as soon as practicable, put into permanent and obtainable form the excellent lectures he had been wont to deliver to the students. This address he feelingly responded to, tendering his gratitude to the brethren, and promising to do what he could to fulfil their request for the publication of his lectures. The members of the Committee for the Didsbury Branch of the Theological Institution expressed to him similar sentiments; and with testimonial offerings from themselves and friends, Messrs. Heald, Kay, Napier, and many others, contributed at once over £2,000 for a new house to be erected for his successor, which Miss Heald generously furnished, in order that during the remainder of life he and his invalid wife might not be disturbed in their dwelling, but continue there as long as God should spare the life of either of them. The students at Didsbury presented to him an excellent and elaborate time-piece, as their token of gratitude for his services to them; while the students of the last and of former years joined in the request that he would as soon as convenient sit to John Adams, Esq., the sculptor, for a marble bust, to be placed for them in the hall at Didsbury. The Conference granted the request, made through the District-Committee, that Dr. HANNAH should leave the office of Theological Tutor and become a supernumerary; expressing to him by the President, and the voluntary tributes of several of its members, as also by formal and special resolution in its Journal and Minutes, its high appreciation of his character and services. His acknowledgments, at the Conference as elsewhere, were modest, grateful, and affectionate; and after the Conference he returned to his peaceful abode on the Institution-grounds at Didsbury, where almost immediately he commenced writing out his lectures for publication, in fulfilment of the request of his brethren.

He was still the willing preacher of the Gospel, as far as circumstances would allow; and still the tender and devoted pastor of the sick, as well as of the members of his class, which he had been accustomed to meet. And still, as in former times, he was the instructive and consoling correspondent to friends who needed seasonable counsel and sympathy. Few men have had more personal attached friends than Dr. HANNAH; and few men have been more regular and attentive in correspondence than he. The large number of students who had received theological instruction from him, and the numerous persons with whom he had become acquainted through public religious services conducted by him in different parts of the kingdom, with his deep sympathy for the bereaved and sorrowful, entailed upon him much letter-writing. He was formed for *friendship*. His tender, loving nature sought reciprocal affection and congenial tastes and feelings. In one sense, friendship was the staff of his life; and where he had proved that he could do so securely, he leaned upon it with unhesitating confidence, expressing his inmost thoughts, and various feelings of anxiety, joy, or sorrow, without reserve. Socially, he was a warm-hearted, happy man. He entered the house of a friend, and sprang forth to meet him, and to grasp his hand there, or elsewhere, with more than youthful ardour. And having once made a friend, it may be safely affirmed that he never lost one; for friendship with him could only strengthen with increased acquaintance and advance of time. He was chivalrous in defence of an absent friend, if spoken against; and, as in his boyhood, when to save a companion from drowning he plunged headlong into a deep river, though he could not swim, so in manhood and Christian maturity, he would have died for a friend.

In the early part of December last he came on a visit to my house in London, where he remained nearly a fortnight; during which time Mr. Adams modelled from his fine, impressive head an excellent classical bust, which, in future, will fitly represent him as he appeared towards the end of life. Mr. Green's half-length portrait of him in the Centenary Hall represents him in middle life. He was then a large, fine man. In figure he was upright, except a graceful bend of the head, and nearly six feet high. His countenance, when in repose, was devoutly thoughtful and impressive, but readily kindled into an expression of cheerfulness; and, though dark in complexion, became at times radiant with joy. His dark eyes were deeply sunk under thick shaggy brows, which in former years—with his long flowing hair turned over the crown of his head and behind the ears—were raven black, but had become grey with age. His gentle and measured step was in accordance with his deep sense of propriety in demeanour; so that, ordinarily, he was solemn and respectful in all his movements. He was remarkably neat and orderly in his dress. Clothed in black, of somewhat primitive shape,—with broad white neckerchief,—he was at once simple and dignified in appearance; so that a stranger on seeing him would conclude that he was no ordinary man, and that he was a venerable minister of Christ. In fact, he might well have been taken for a dignitary of the Church. In youth, with his thick black overhanging hair and eyebrows, and when his limbs were not fully formed and set, he was somewhat "ungainly" in appearance. And though, in the time of war, when the Lincoln Militia had to be elsewhere, Dr. Hannah in true loyalty joined the rank and file with the volunteers, and in military clothing appeared on parade-ground and for drill; yet, withal, by the testimony of those who remember his youth, he was at that period hardly equal in look and gait to blooming, pliant young men in general. But in matured life he was comely and gentlemanly in his aspect and demeanour; and advancing age, with its attendant growth and maturity in goodness, softened down all harshness of the features, and mellowed them into peaceful and reverential repose. Mr.

Adams's admirable bust shows this, and preserves for our grateful remembrance the dignified head and expressive countenance of the deceased.

After standing or sitting half an hour for this bust in my study, where friends conversed freely with him, he expressed surprise at the sense of weariness that came upon him. And before this, even on his arrival, both Mrs. Jobson and I perceived a change in his appearance, and that he was not in his usual state of health. At times he was buoyantly cheerful. He was ready for conversation; and, as on previous occasions, we read and conversed together on subjects of passing interest,—he quoting aptly, as wont, both poetry and prose. We read, piecemeal and successively, as opportunity allowed, the several essays of a volume which brought forth for review most of the leading questions disturbing and endangering the Protestant Church at this time, both of Ritualism and Popery on the one hand, and of Rationalistic latitudinarianism on the other. This drew out his views on doctrinal and ecclesiastical subjects distinctively and decisively. He was a firm supporter of law and order. And he had deep reverence for established things that good and great men had been connected with. His very education and training in the grand old city of Lincoln, crowded with ancient churches, and crowned on "its sovereign hill" with its majestic cathedral, would, upon his thoughtful, reverential mind, tend to produce this. As an intelligent Wesleyan, read in ecclesiastical history, and in the struggles for the Reformation by champions in the Church of England, who died martyrs for the truth, he venerated the Establishment of the land, and desired its real welfare. But the attempts to revive for it obsolete forms, and to introduce Popish rites and ceremonies, roused his wrathful indignation, and led him to declare that they who did such things were traitors to the cause they professed to have espoused, and that they ought at once to be cast out. In his earlier ministry he used, at baptism, to sign the infant, after ancient form, with the sign of the cross; but when in later life he found that such signs were abused to the favour of Popery, he ceased from using the sign, and, with the accompanying prayers and thanksgivings, simply sprinkled the child with water in the name of the Father, the Son, and the Holy Ghost. He was impatient under the speculations of Rationalism. He beheld in them want of submission to the authority of God in His word; and traced sceptical doubt of Divine Revelation, not only to the mind, but, as God Himself does, to the heart.

Upon questions vital to Methodism he had cheerful confidence. Having retired, himself, from the front rank of service, he did not spend his time in looking for false steps in those whom he had left. He rejoiced in the belief that the students at Didsbury would find in his amiable and accomplished successor, the Rev. William Burt Pope, a safe and a successful instructor; and he was not less hopeful for the Theological Institution because he himself had ceased to be officially connected with it. He had undiminished confidence in it, and in other departments of Methodism. On one or two points relating to the rising ministry among us he was anxious, and at times expressed deep concern. One was, lest the young men recommended for it should not be equal, in mental capacity and earnest diligence, to the candidates for our ministry in past times. He said that, from observation on this matter, he thought that on this ground there was reason for anxiety and fear; and that, whether through increased attractions in the world for intelligent energetic young men, or want of equal devotedness to Christ, or from both these reasons, it seemed to be a fact, that, in mental calibre and impulsive energy, the young men entering our ministry now are not equal to the young men who entered it in past years. And, as he observed, inferior minds, with the best theological education and training, never can rise into superior or even mediocre preachers of Christ and ministers of His church. "Give me," exclaimed he, energetically, when speaking on this topic, "a ploughboy with a mind like John Hunt, one of my first students, and I would prefer him, ten thousand times over, to an educated and accomplished weakling."

Another subject of concern with him was the *preaching* of young Methodist ministers. He feared lest, tempted by straining after novel forms of expression, and after the finished periods and gaudy adornments of rhetoricians, the full simplicity of the Gospel should be lost and forfeited. He knew how to appreciate the really sound and beautiful; and few men had stronger relish for real poetic clothing than he had. But the crude and grotesque imitations for which men labour, and which they strain their ingenuity to obtain and to elaborate, he nauseated, as every well-regulated mind must do. When professionally addressing his students on this topic, he used to say earnestly, "Preach the old-fashioned Gospel, in the old-fashioned way." And when speaking of this a few days before his death, he said to me, "I sometimes hear a sermon that distresses me. I cannot say it is a new Gospel; but it is a new dress, or new sound for it; and I have to ponder to know if it be really the Jerusalem Gospel I have been familiar with. I like," said he, with zest, "to hear the old ring of the old Gospel." I name these anxieties and solicitudes of the departed, not that we may go to and fro mopishly expressing our fears, or crying down into weakness our rising ministry; but that we may do as our departed friend did,—make them the subjects of earnest prayer before God, supplicating Him, of His infinite mercy, to give us men for our ministry of the true stamp, mentally and morally.

During his last sojourn with me, he spoke much of the past, and of his associations with Lincoln. He might almost be said to have then reviewed his life for me. He traced his ministerial course, dwelling fondly on the scenes of his earlier services, and on his former friendships and alliances, both in the ministry and among the laity. He spoke at length of his stations at Nottingham, Leeds, Manchester, and Huddersfield; and of the favour shown to him in those Circuits. Of his ministerial colleagues and friends in Manchester he spoke with special interest; relating several incidents which had evidently impressed him deeply. One was the real nobility evinced by Dr. Bunting and the Rev. Richard Watson, his colleagues in the Manchester Third Circuit, when they met in his house after differences between them on some public questions, concerning which they had taken decided and antagonistic positions. He had invited them to dinner at his table, not knowing what the meeting would be. From what had previously passed under a sense of public duty, it might have been supposed that they would have met frowning darkly at each other, like two thunder-clouds. But, instead of that, they met not only courteously, but fraternally, each giving the other full credit for sincerity and conscientiousness.

His reverence for these two great men was profound, and he never referred to them without showing it to be so. As an accurate and safe theologian; as a clear, lucid, and powerful preacher; and as a liberal, large-minded administrator for the scriptural government of the church of God, he declared Dr. Bunting to have been, in his opinion, the greatest man he had known; while the Doctor's urbanity, sociability, and fatherly attentions to his colleagues, had evidently impressed him most favourably. Mr. Watson he viewed as having possessed the loftiest intellect he had known; and he referred to him as the impersonation of solemn majestic thought. He spoke, also, of the Rev. Theophilus Lessey, as among the most pathetic and eloquent preachers he had heard; as, also, of Mr. William Dawson, with whom he had been personally associated in Leeds, and of the style, and of the effects produced by the preaching, of that dramatic and effective Yorkshire genius. Usually, he did not in conversation dwell so much upon the men of the past, as upon what might be hoped for from those rising up and coming forth to be the men of the future. He was naturally less disposed to build sepulchres for the prophets, than to raise up living stones for the spiritual house of the Most High. But at this time he made affecting references, again and again, to the dead in Christ whom he had known and loved; and he did so with great zest and manifest enjoyment.

Nor was LINCOLN, his native city, forgotten or unnamed. It ever lived in his memory; and, journey or visit where he would, he bore the remembrance of it fondly in his mind. He spoke of it as he knew it in his youth, with its former generation of Methodists; and of the few that remain who were fellow-worshippers and workers with him when he was stationed in it. You remember his yearly visits and ministrations among you; and though, for the most part, the sons and daughters of his contemporaries, yet you have never ceased to venerate him as a father in Christ. You know that it was my privilege to be associated with him here in social and public services; and last July, you will remember, we were with you together for your chapel-anniversary. We preached alternately in this pulpit on the Sunday, and on Monday evening attended a social meeting that filled the lower part of this large and commodious place of worship. We had spent the day in revisiting old scenes. The cathedral, with its solemn aisles and stately towers, had been again surveyed by us. We had looked again upon the Roman gate of ancient LINDUM; and, just before coming to the evening meeting, we walked in company to Monks' Abbey, and, between its crumbling, picturesque ruins and surrounding elms, we watched the sun as he glowed in golden descent behind the elevated minster, appearing in deep, massive, purple shadow towards us; and, as we trod the heaps of buried walls, we spoke of the probable scenes that in former days had there been witnessed, and of the light-hearted, gleesome feelings with which we had scrambled about its ruins in our respective boyhoods.

In the meeting here, as you will call to mind, Dr. Hannah spoke of early Methodism in Lincoln; related what had been done for it by holy women, for which he said, emphatically, Lincoln Methodism had been distinguished from the beginning, down from the days of Sarah Parrot, of Bracebridge,—who by prayerful importunity brought Mrs. Fisher, from Gonerby, to it, to build the first Methodist chapel and to entertain itinerant ministers,—through the days of Mrs. Bavin, Mary Proudlove, and my own dear mother, to the present time. He was truly at home, and happy among us at that, the last meeting he attended here. Indeed, his niece relates, in particulars furnished for this service, that he returned home from it affirming that the meeting was the happiest he had ever spent with dear friends on earth. And his son, Dr. John Hannah, in kindly supplying me with notes on his father's connection with Lincoln, and on the events and incidents of his father's life, observes, voluntarily and truly, " He was loved and honoured at Lincoln from first to last; and there was no place and no circle of friends for which he cherished a warmer affection." I should rather understate than overstate the extent of Dr. HANNAH's reminiscences of Lincoln when we were last together, if I were to say that, of the twelve days he spent with me in London, he occupied altogether as much as one entire day in speaking of it.

On appearing at breakfast one morning, the Doctor looked worn and serious. He complained that he had not slept during the night, and that his breathing had been somewhat heavy and difficult. He seemed cheered with his dear wife's epistle, delivered by the morning-post, and said he had no doubt that the day would find him improved in health as it advanced. I remained at home with him that day; and after dinner persuaded him—in consideration of the sleepless night—to rest himself in the easy chair by the fire. He soon fell asleep; but the sounds of short, ruttling breath alarmed me; and though, when he woke up, he declared confidently, that he was himself again, I remained anxious and fearful. After a day or two he seemed to have nearly recovered his usual state of health; but as the Sabbath approached, he said to me, "You will be expecting that we shall do on Sunday as we have before done when together,—divide the services of the day; but you must not ask me to preach, for I do not feel really equal to doing so. I shall go with you both times, and we will worship together." I replied, "As you are not strong, I will not ask you to preach for me. I shall be at Mildmay-Park chapel in the morning, and at Highbury chapel in the evening. But as there are notable preachers within reach, I would advise you to hear one of them, at least." "No," he rejoined; "I shall go with you. I like to be with my friends, and to worship among my own people." He was with me throughout that day; neither of us thinking that it was to be the last Sabbath we were to spend together on earth. Little thought he or I, as we stood up at the beginning of

Sunday-morning worship, that three weeks hence at that hour he would pass from earth to the worship of heaven. It was, however, in our ignorance of the future, and by Divine blessing, a happy day: we called the Sabbath a delight, and we felt it to be holy of the Lord and honourable. He remained through the week; and, as Mrs. Hannah encouraged him by her communications to do so, he stayed to accompany me by the North Western train, as I should have to go on Saturday afternoon, December 14, to Burslem; and he would thus be able to travel with me most of the way towards his own home. We travelled together as far as Stafford, where we separated; he going directly forward by Crewe to Stockport, and I turning off on the line to the Potteries. Before leaving him, I saw him safely seated in a warm, comfortable carriage, wrapped up in his large cape; he assuring me that he had there all that he desired. His train glided away, and we waved hands, and parted for ever on earth.

On reaching home, Dr. Hannah complained that cold was still upon him; and on the day following he remained at home, worshipping there as circumstances allowed. He had an appointment for Oxford-road chapel, Manchester, that morning; but, feeling his weakness and incapability, he had written from town to his friend the Rev. William Jackson, the Governor of the Didsbury Institution, to supply the pulpit for him by the best student that could be selected at the time. So that the service he had at the opening of the new chapel at Walsall—when he preached there on Monday, November 25, with great pathos and power, from Rev. xxii. 17, "And the Spirit and the bride say, Come. And let him that heareth say, Come. And let him that is athirst come. And whosoever will, let him take the water of life freely"—was the last public service in which he officiated. In the early part of the week, immediately after his return home, he continued unwell. On Thursday, December 19, he went into the meeting of the Committee for the Didsbury Institution, when he felt chill, seemed to his friends there restless and uneasy, and soon left the Committee meeting and went home, saying to Mrs. Hannah as he entered her room, "My place is not in the College, but here." The President of the Conference, the Rev. John Bedford, followed him home, and conversed with him in his study, when he complained of cold which he had felt upon him for some time; but he spoke cheerfully on several subjects. Afterwards he retired to his bed, from which he never rose again; and gradually sank so low that medical counsel declared, unless there was very speedy relief, the result would be serious. These apprehensions, in which he shared, did not alarm him. He quietly committed himself to God in Christ, and trusted unwaveringly in Him. In his last sickness he was greatly consoled by the visits and attentions of his colleagues.

On Friday, December 27, as a lady who had visited him was departing, he said to her, "Good bye. Give my love to your children, to each of them; and tell them that the blood of Jesus is enough for me now, and that it will be enough for them for everything." On that day his niece, Miss Parker, for whom he cared with fatherly tenderness of affection, said to him, "Jesus is very precious." DR. HANNAH replied instantly and with emphasis, "O yes! O yes!" By the evening of that Friday his son, Dr. John Hannah, Warden of Glenalmond College, Perthshire,—in whom he had just pride and delight, as an accomplished scholar and a devoted clergyman,—arrived, to watch and minister at his bedside, which was a real solace to him. On Saturday the President of the Conference, learning his critical state, again visited him, and found him much changed in appearance. He gave fraternal greeting to the President; and when the President, after words of consolation, briefly prayed with him, again and again he responded, "Amen! Amen!" Then firmly grasping the President's hand, he looked up with eyes beaming with calm and joyous hope, and gently whispered, "My dear friend, Jesus is mine; all is well." Mr. Napier saw him almost immediately afterwards; and to him he said, "My dear friend, all is well. I shall soon be where the weary are for ever at rest." On that day his beloved niece had quoted to him the opening of the passage in the book of Nahum: "The Lord is good, a strong hold in the day of trouble;" when he finished the verse, adding, "and He knoweth them that trust in Him." Some time afterwards she said, while moistening his lips with water, "You will soon drink of the water of life." He replied immediately, "That was my last"—meaning "text," which he could not then utter. He sent me on the morning of that day a last message of affection. In the afternoon of the day he was thought to be dying: his son knelt down by him, and prayed fervently; to which prayer the father responded by emphatic "Amens." Mrs. Hannah sent from her bed in the study, to which she had been that day removed, a tender message of love to him; to which he promptly responded, though scarcely able to articulate, by requesting that Mrs. Hannah's favourite psalm, the twenty-third, "The Lord is my Shepherd," &c., and her favourite hymn, commencing,

"Thou Shepherd of Israel and mine,"

might be read to him. They were read to him accordingly; and he whispered again and again, as they were read, "Amen!" This whispered "Amen" was the last word heard from him. After this he took little notice of anything; only now and then opening his eyes towards his son, and his son's wife, who ministered attentively to him; and on the next morning, December 29, 1867, which was that of the Lord's day, just as the service was commenced in the chapel adjoining, where he had so often worshipped on earth, he passed to the worship and service of heaven.

Tidings of Dr. Hannah's death spread rapidly through the kingdom, and produced surprise and sorrow among thousands. The hope had been generally entertained, that he would pass some remaining years at Didsbury in undisturbed repose; and that he would still be able to give partial counsel and service to the Connexion, as they might be called for. But the Divine Being had, in infinite wisdom, ordered it otherwise. And, considering his temperament, and his habit of leaning upon others, entirely, in temporal arrangements and provisions, his friends can see under the heavy stroke of bereavement that has fallen upon them, that it was, nevertheless, "goodness and mercy" from the Lord to His servant in thus suddenly removing him from earth to heaven. He himself had become apprehensive of loneliness and discomfort, if left as the survivor of his wife. This, however, his friends were not thinking of; and when the news of his departure was received by them, they mourned their own loss, and the loss sustained by his family, and by Methodism at large. Many clad themselves voluntarily in mourning; numerous letters of sympathy with the afflicted widow were sent to her; pulpits in which he had been wont to minister were covered with signs of his death; and preachers in different parts of the kingdom referred to him with deep emotion.

His funeral at Didsbury on Thursday, January 2, 1868, was very numerously attended. Though it took place in the depth of winter, at some miles distance from any populous town, and in a comparatively secluded village, there was an attendance of friends from London, Bristol, Birmingham, Leeds, Huddersfield, Macclesfield, Southport, Liverpool, Bury, Summerseat, Manchester, Stockport, and other parts of the kingdom; so that, altogether, not less than one thousand persons assembled to pay to his memory the last earthly tribute of respectful and affectionate homage.

The religious service in the Institution-chapel, crowded in every part, was most solemn and impressive. The body of the deceased was placed in front of the communion-rails; and on the pall that covered it was a chaplet-wreath of white flowers, supplied by affection which exulted in the assurance of his conquest, through Christ, over sin and death. Several ministers, known to have been immediate friends and associates of Dr. Hannah, took the several parts of the service; viz., the Revs. William W. Stamp, John D. Geden, William Jackson, William B. Pope, and John Rattenbury, and myself. The Rev. John Bedford, President of the Conference, and who for many years had been connected with him in friendly and official co-operation, delivered a beautiful, comprehensive, and affecting address on Dr. Hannah's character and services. Under its delivery there were gushing outbursts of feeling that could not be suppressed. The Revs. Dr. Osborn, an attached friend through many years,—and John Farrar, Secretary of the Conference, also a personal friend, as well as his former colleague both in Circuit-service and in tutorship in the Theological Institution,—added most appropriate and touching utterances. And the singing, the reading of the Scriptures, and the prayers, on that occasion were all reverentially devout and sabbatic in their character. Gratitude to God for the life, example, and memory of one so pure and heavenly, mingled with affectionate sorrow, both of his family and friends present. And though the sacred service was sad and mournful in one aspect, yet it was blessed in thankfulness and joyful in hope, so as to be fully in accordance with the character of the deceased, and was a real means of spiritual benefit to all.

The following paragraph, which appeared next week in a Wesleyan journal, describes the funeral itself:—

"It had been arranged that the interment should take place in the burying-ground belonging to Didsbury church, where DR. HANNAH owned a family-grave; and accordingly a solemn procession of sorrowing friends now formed at the door of his late residence, and moved on with their precious dead towards the church close by. The procession was headed by the officiating clergymen, the Rev. William J. Kidd, Rector of Didsbury, and the Rev. Charles C. Bluett, M.A., Incumbent of Barlow-Moor, followed by Messrs. Ockleston and Bannerman—the former DR. HANNAH's medical attendant; by the President and Secretary of the Conference; by the Rev. John Lomas, the Rev. W. W. Stamp, the Rev. John Rattenbury, and the Rev. Dr. Osborn, Ex-Presidents of the Conference; and the Rev. Messrs. Jackson, Pope, and Geden. After these came the Body, carried by eight members of the Methodist Society at Didsbury, the pall being borne by the Rev. Peter M'Owan, the Rev. Dr. Jobson, and Messrs. William R. Johnson, T. Percival Bunting, John Chubb, John Fernley, John Napier, and George Marsden. DR. HANNAH's family was represented by his son, the Rev. John Hannah, D.C.L., Warden of Glenalmond College, Perthshire; by his grandson, the Rev. Julius Hannah, B.A., late of Balliol College, Oxford; and by Mr. Sharples, of Tamworth. Behind the chief mourners followed a train of not fewer than a hundred ministers, together with a great number of lay gentlemen from Manchester, Liverpool, Stockport, Birmingham, Bristol, London, and other towns of the kingdom, far and near. Thus, amidst every possible demonstration of grief and honour on the part of the inhabitants of the neighbourhood, the procession made its way to the church. The church was filled to overflowing during the reading of the Burial Service; and never, probably, did such a sorrowing multitude—numbering altogether, as was reckoned, nearly a thousand persons—gather in the churchyard as when the Rector devoutly and feelingly committed to the dust the dear remains of JOHN HANNAH, the glory

K

and beauty of Didsbury, and the object of the universal love and reverence of Methodism at home and abroad. Large as was the attendance at the funeral, it would have been abundantly larger, had not distance, important previous engagements, and personal or family affliction hindered many from being present."

Dr. Hannah's death was officially improved by the President of the Conference, in Oldham-street chapel, Manchester, on Wednesday evening, January 22, to a crowded and most attentive congregation, comprising ministers and friends from all parts of Manchester and its surrounding towns.

Thus was the devoted and faithful servant of Christ honoured in death as well as in life, and the Divine promise, so aptly quoted for him by Dr. Osborn, obtained in him open and public fulfilment: "Because he hath set his love upon Me, therefore will I deliver him: I will set him on high, because he hath known My name. He shall call upon Me, and I will answer him: I will be with him in trouble; I will deliver him, and honour him. With long life will I satisfy him, and show him My salvation."

In seeking PRACTICAL IMPROVEMENT of the event we have met to commemorate, reflections and lessons are numerous.

1. We observe, WHAT REAL GRANDEUR THERE IS IN A LIFE OF ENTIRE DEVOTEDNESS TO CHRIST! We see this in St. John, the beloved disciple; and we see it in our fellow-citizen and friend, recently departed. Suppose JOHN HANNAH had been disobedient to the heavenly call, and, from worldly, selfish views, had remained to occupy—as parental solicitude had thought he would—his father's place, and carry on his father's business in this city, with means and facilities promising to him; and suppose he had succeeded to establish himself in prosperous and wealthy merchandise; what would have been his position and memory, compared with what they are now? They would have been low and mean, comparatively. And he would have borne with him through life, by day and by night, a condemnatory sense of unfaithfulness, which in death—when the world is stripped of its false appearances, and naked realities present themselves—would

have ripened into dread remorse. Could he then have exclaimed in exhaustive weakness, "All is well! I shall soon be where the weary are for ever at rest?" To say nothing of his entrance into the presence of his Lord; or of the joy that awaits him at the resurrection of the just, when "the righteous shall shine as the sun, and they that have turned many to righteousness as the stars for ever and ever;" to speak only of this world, where exalted greatness is assigned to devoted service, and where a man becomes "chief" by being "the servant of all," how surpassingly honourable in life is he who wholly surrenders himself to the Saviour, that he may *be* good and *do* good! What royal alliance could have ennobled DR. HANNAH as much as he was ennobled by his devotedness to Christ and His cause? God set him on high, even among the princes of Israel. Men yielded him reverential homage wherever he appeared in life; and now that he is dead they bless his memory, as having been one of the best inhabitants of earth, who by prayer and praise linked it daily with heaven, and who by disinterested service for others through prolonged years was one of the highest and most apostolic benefactors to mankind. "The memory of the just is blessed; but the name of the wicked shall rot!" The memory of the just is fragrant and pleasant; but the name of the wicked is corrupt and offensive. What a motive to entire surrender of heart and life to Jesus have we in this beloved disciple! What a motive especially have the young ministers among us,—those who have, as we reckon, a life to consecrate to the service of God and to their generation by His will! All may not be so gifted and endowed mentally as Dr. Hannah. Few are so. But all that will may be as good and as faithful as he; and all that will may meet Christ with joy at His coming, and have a glorious reward. Let the event we now commemorate, in relation to him whom we knew and revered, stimulate and lead to this. *Then* his death, any more than his life, shall not be in vain in the Lord.

2. Another reflection suggested by the deep loss sustained in the removal of our father and friend is,—OUR ENTIRE AND, IN ONE SENSE, OUR HELPLESS DEPENDENCE UPON GOD FOR THE SUPPLY OF SUITABLE AND EFFICIENT LABOURERS IN HIS CAUSE. We have lost from among us a devoted and honoured servant of the Saviour. Our vineyard has in it a labourer less. "The field, which is the world," has been deprived of one who not only ploughed and sowed, but who reaped largely. The hosts of the Lord have lost a champion and a leader who was "valiant for the truth," and his fall in the conflict is "as when a standard-bearer fainteth." Who shall supply his place? Who shall be baptized for the dead? We cannot fill it, or put another into it. The Lord of the harvest alone can send forth labourers. The God of battles alone can bring forth soldiers for the Cross. "Pray ye therefore the Lord of the harvest, that He will send forth" more "labourers into His harvest." Cry to God that He would raise up men of might, and that He would "teach

their hands to war and their fingers to fight," so that they may "do valiantly."

Our princes are falling one after another,—the men who scorned self-seeking, and who, though they obtained position and honour, did not seek either, but humbly and disinterestedly held and sustained the distinctions conferred on them, not for themselves, but for the glory of Him who had called and exalted them. They were kings and priests among good men, possessing a royal spirit that ennobled and elevated them to universal homage. Of late, the brighter lights of our ministry, who shed distinguished lustre upon our Connexion, have been successively quenched, until we tremblingly ask if the glory is departing from us. Little more than a year ago, Dr. HANNAH publicly improved for us the death of a mutual and beloved friend, the REV. WILLIAM MACLARDIE BUNTING, who—for bright intelligence, refined culture, sprightly conversation, evangelical preaching, devotional hymn-writing, pastoral diligence, and large-hearted catholic sympathies—has seldom been surpassed. Since this year commenced, we have lost by death the sagacious, persistent, and successful Principal of our Normal Training College at Westminster, the Rev. John Scott; who, wise in counsel, skilful in management, and devoted to Methodism, sought continuously the glory of God and the highest good of mankind. He not only promoted established institutions for ministers and people among us, at home and abroad, but, under Divine guidance and blessing, himself created and brought into prosperous working an educational establishment which commands national attention; and which has extended its agencies by sending forth since its commencement more than a thousand trained and certificated teachers to our Week-day Schools in different parts of the kingdom, and some of them to the very ends of the earth. And Dr. Hannah, the safe and efficient instructor and trainer of our rising ministers, has also been removed from us.

These, and others of our departed fathers

and brethren that might be named, were disinterested, generous, able leaders among us who, while devoted to their own community, sought that great grace might be with all who love the Lord Jesus Christ. They were simple-minded, soul-saving Methodist preachers; loyal to established order and government, both in the Church and in the nation; true Wesleyans, practically, as well as professedly,—"the friends of all, and the enemies of none." Shall their successors be like them? We stand here to-day on this side of the Jordan they have crossed, and, looking wistfully up towards our departed leaders, we cry, "My father! my father! the chariot of Israel, and the horsemen thereof." Shall the spirit of our ascended Elijahs be found upon the Elishas left among us? Shall unselfish, devoted service to God and His cause, seeking only to save souls, as our Founder enjoined upon his helpers, characterize the men who shall press to the front among us and become influential leaders to our ministers and people? Or shall noisy partisanship, seeking place and power among disturbers of what is settled, and among open agitators for revolution and change, appear?

If the latter, then the strength of Israel shall have departed from us, and the various, complicated, and ponderous machinery of Methodist agency,— having wheel within wheel, and which moves with full-eyed intelligence and noiseless order so long as the Spirit be in the midst of it,—no longer supported by Almighty power, fall by its own weight, and become a proverb and a bye-word to the church and the world. But should simple, unostentatious, soul-saving Methodism hold on its way, after the example of the past; and, amidst smiles and frowns, rebukes and solicitations, "ask for the old paths," and "walk in them," then shall her future be more illustrious than the past; and she shall go forth against ungodliness and sin,—against Popish encroachments on the one hand, and rationalistic infidelity on the other,—"fair as the moon, clear as the sun, and terrible as an army with banners." Let us earnestly pray and diligently labour for this; and then shall the departures of our beloved friends and brethren be improved by us as intended by Him who says, "I am He that liveth, and was dead; and, behold, I am alive for evermore, Amen; and have the keys of hell and of death." Then shall we joyfully realize the truth of the voice from heaven which proclaims, " Blessed are the dead which die in the Lord from henceforth : Yea, saith the Spirit, that they may rest from their labours; and their works do follow them." God grant it may be so!— and to Him be all honour and glory, now and evermore. Amen.

BY THE SAME AUTHOR.

AUSTRALIA: WITH NOTES BY THE WAY, ON EGYPT, CEYLON, BOMBAY, AND THE HOLY LAND. With a Coloured Illustration. Third Edition. Crown 8vo., 3s. 6d.
Fine copy, cambric, gilt, 6s.

AMERICA, AND AMERICAN METHODISM: WITH A PREFATORY LETTER BY THE REV. JOHN HANNAH, D.D. Illustrated from Original Sketches by the Author. Crown 8vo., ornamented cloth, 7s. 6d.

SAVING TRUTHS. Third Edition. 18mo., cloth, gilt lettered. Price 1s. 6d.

CHAPEL AND SCHOOL ARCHITECTURE. With numerous Plates and Illustrations. Octavo, 8s.

A MOTHER'S PORTRAIT. With Twenty Engravings on Wood, from Original Pictures by JAMES SMETHAM and FREDERICK J. JOBSON. Crown 8vo., 5s.

THE SERVANT OF HIS GENERATION: A TRIBUTE TO THE MEMORY OF THE REV. JABEZ BUNTING, D.D. Crown 8vo., 4s. embossed and gilt; 3s. plain.

THE SHIPWRECKED MINISTER, AND HIS DROWNING CHARGE. MEMORIAL TRIBUTE TO THE REV. DANIEL J. DRAPER. Price 1s.

www.ingramcontent.com/pod-product-compliance
Lightning Source LLC
Chambersburg PA
CBHW030357170426
43202CB00010B/1402